"The Lord bless you
and keep you;
The Lord make
His face shine
upon you,
And be gracious
to you;
The Lord lift up
His countenance
upon you,
And give you
peace."

Numbers 6:24-26 (NKJV)

With love to:

———————————————

From:

———————————————

DECREE, DECLARE, CONFESS, & AGREE

EXPOSING 21 LIES

of the enemy of your soul.
Applying God's truth to them
& securing a relationship with God
in the process.

Breathed by: The Ruach HaKodesh
Through: Yolanda Nichols

Exposing 21 lies of the enemy of your soul.

Applying God's truth to them and

securing a relationship with God in the process;

A personal Bible study

with Decrees, Declarations,

Godly Confessions,

and Agreements of His Word.

You have Word Power.

Now is your time to use it.

Breathed by: The Ruach HaKodesh

Through: Yolanda Nichols

Disclaimer: Please take note, while every attempt has been made to verify that no copyright infringements occur, we respect the right to make corrections as needed. We respect the right to make modifications, revisions, updates, and changes as the true Holy Spirit leads. Remember, we are all continually going from glory to glory. All information is for informational and teaching purposes. It is not intended to substitute a medical or professional consult. Please consult a professional before engaging in any fast. At the time of this publication, all links, phone numbers, addresses, and information were accurate. All images, graphics, and fonts are free from copyright infringements. Bible versions have been copyright addressed. Facts and events may be altered to protect everyone. This is non-fiction work. However, it is recognized that some people may have different memories. This writing is not meant to hurt anyone but to establish a baseline from the author's point of view. If you feel there is an error, please notify the author at the address provided above. As the Body of Christ, we do not slander, gossip, violate copyright infringements, and we strongly believe in the healthy unity of the body. Together we advance the Kingdom of Yâhh. Also, the enemy of humanity, aka satan, has been addressed as the enemy of your soul. Against grammatical errors, we will not capitalize nor address the entity by its human name. Thank you! We walk, live by faith, and not by our sight.[i]

Printed in the United States of America

ISBN 13: 9780578637402

All honor and all glory to our
Lord Yeshua HaMashiach!

Inside You Will Find

Section One: Laying Down The Foundation

You yourselves write a decree concerning the Jews,
as you please, in the King's name, and seal it with the
King's signet ring;
for whatever is written in the King's name and sealed
with the King's signet ring no one can revoke.
Esther 8:8 (NKJV)

Our responsibility

Authors of the Bible were faithful by writing down their thoughts, passions, failures, victories, and their relationship with God[1]. They were obedient authors. They did not worry about book sales or critics. Their only objective was to obey and heed the Lord.

Like them, we have a responsibility and duty. It is our duty and responsibility to publish the message He has delivered through us for His people. We must overcome all fears and obstacles because it is not about us but the directive of our Father. We are mere instruments of His doing. He has birthed a message in all of us. So we must see it delivered. We must ask ourselves if our motive is to make money or deliver His message and be obedient children.

Having said that, if you have not accepted Jesus Christ as your savior, here are some quick questions to ask yourself. Why did I wake up today? For what reason do I exist? Where is my life going? For a detailed description of why you need to be saved, turn to page #127. Through Jesus Christ, you will find the answers. Even more, the study will become more apparent to you. To accept Jesus Christ into your life, please read page #24 and do this before beginning the study.

If you have surrendered your life to Jesus Christ, I pray you enjoy the ride and allow the Lord Jesus Christ to speak to you on an even deeper level. Allow Him to take you deeper than you are right now. Deeper into His presence. Deeper Into His being.

---

1   *You will find the names of God used in this study on Section 3 page 190.*

How to use this book

As with any Bible study, you will need your Bible, a notebook, highlighters, and a pen. But mostly you just need to have an open mind. If you browse through this study and immediately discredit it or me, the author, or even glimpse at it to find mistakes, you've already placed fear and doubt inside of you. Fear and doubt will hinder your ability to grow spiritually. So leave all religious preconceptions at the door. I'm not saying there are no errors in the study because I, the writer, am an imperfect person. I'm not asking you to agree with me 100%. I'm asking you to trust God's process in you thru this book. What I'm saying is for you to have an open mind and allow The Holy Spirit to guide you, lead you, teach you, and train you through this study.

Here's a suggestion, first, skim through the book. Make yourself comfortable with the material. Second, read up to "Stop!" Then, when you are ready to dive into the daily studies, do so. Go at your own pace. Seriously, pace yourself. There's no rush. You are in control of the studying process. As a suggestion, you may use this book during your time with the Lord.

For example, seeking God first thing in the morning is like receiving "manna"[2] from heaven. The Lord provides afresh in the mornings. Equally, quail[3] is reserved for the evenings. The Lord satiates in the evenings. But make sure to give yourself enough time to heal through the process of this study. The Lord will guide you if you let Him. He takes care of the faithful. Those who are hungry for more of Him.

---

2   Exodus 16:14 (NKJV) [14] And when the layer of dew lifted, there, on the surface of the wilderness, was a small round substance, as fine as frost on the ground.

3   Psalm 105:40 (NKJV) [40] The people asked, and He brought quail, And satisfied them with the bread of heaven.

A Common Question

You are probably asking yourself, "What if I don't hear the voice of God?" First, I wrote this book for everyday folks. Much of the "theological, religious, self-righteous, pious" language has been purposefully reduced, to the best of my ability. I want you to be able to hear the Spirit talking to you directly. I want you to feel confident that you hear His voice. Remember, we are all the same. We're His children. No one is better than anyone. We can all hear the voice of the Good Shepherd if we are quiet enough. That's the only caveat, to hearing the voice of God, we must be still, we must quiet ourselves. Let's read Matthew 7:7 in the amplified version.

> ### Matthew 7:7 (AMP)
>
> [7]"Ask and keep on asking and it will be given to you; seek, and keep on seeking and you will find; knock and keep on knocking, and the door will be opened to you.

What God is saying is that if you ask Him into your heart, He will come in. If you seek Him, He will draw closer to you. If you knock on His door, He will open it and speak. The decrees, declarations, confessions, and agreements in this book will shape your future, free you from your past, and, most importantly, draw you closer to God. So that you can confidently and clearly hear His voice. You can have an intimate personal relationship with Him. You can hear His voice!

> "Into me, God, you see.
> Into you, God, I see."
> ~ Original Author Unknown

If you are not confident, you hear His voice, speak to Him. Peace your soul. Quiet your surroundings. Turn off the internet and the world. Be still and wait. Be still because He is God. He sees it all, and He hears it all. He knows how much you long to hear from Him. He knows your burning heart for Him. He knows you! He knows your innermost parts. He knows things about you that you don't know yet. He knows more about you than you can comprehend. You are His child! His beloved child! He loves you! Warts and all! He has seen you fall and cheers for you when you get back up. He saw your birthday, and He knows your physical end day. He's with you every day of your life.

So, be still, listen, hush your mind. If you need to get away from the world for about 5 minutes, then do that. Start with only 5 minutes. Get in a place where it's just you and Him. It could even be your bathroom. Many of us start in our bathroom. And since we're completely transparent, I sometimes still return to the bathroom for that quiet (get-away) sanctuary. I mean, that's how I began my quiet time with the Lord. I wanted it to be just Him and me. I needed to learn to tune the world out and did not know how to turn it off. So, I often retreated to the bathroom. The only quiet place at the time in my life. Away from my kids, my husband, and the daily grind of motherhood. Sometimes there were endless showers full of tears and even unspoken prayers.

So, you see, as you press in, you will not want to stop talking to Him and listening for His voice. The conversations between you and your Heavenly Father will just flow. He loves to talk to you. He speaks to everyone! EVERYONE! That means you, me, and it means your children. Because of Jesus Christ, we can all speak and hear from God. Christ became that bridge of communication. Long gone are the days when only the privileged could hear from God.

Now, everyone listening with open ears and a willing heart can have a dialogue with Him. Our Father wants to talk to His beloved children. You are His precious and dear child. Of course, He wants to talk to you. Of course, He wants to fellowship with you. Of course, He wants you to hear His voice. He wants you to know that He is still whispering to you. Sometimes audibly, through billboards, signs, songs, texts, books, and sometimes through other people. Yes, sometimes, through social media. He will use everything to pursue you.[ii]

Just listen. Ask Father-God to open your ears to His voice, His presence. He will speak as you listen. He will draw you to His voice as you quiet your voice and your mind. So be still! Stop! Wait!

Daughter or son of Zion,[iii] Abba is waiting for you. He wants to have a conversation with you. He longs to hear your sweet voice. He longs to be with you because He is your loving Daddy. He created you with love and tenderness. You are fearfully and preciously made.[iv] He rejoices over you! He has beautiful thoughts about you and for your future. He has prepared a glorious life for you. Trust Him. Trust His process. Lean on Him.

In contrast, if you have ever sinned and have not accepted Jesus Christ as your personal Lord and Savior, now is the perfect time to do so. Simply repeat the prayer below, with whatever ounce of faith you have, and allow your heart to be surrendered to the leading of The Holy Spirit. This humble prayer is not heretical.[v] It flows from the willingness of your heart to surrender. It says, "I'm done doing it my way. I surrender."

Here are some scriptures that talk about this prayer, also called the sinners' prayer: Romans 3:10; Titus 3:5-7; Matthew 25:46; John 1:1,14; John 8:46; 2 Corinthians 5:21; Romans 5:8, Colossians 2:15; 1 Corinthians 15; Romans 10:9-10; and Ephesians 2:8.

You might want to read over these scriptures before surrendering your life over to the leading of The Holy Spirit. But fear not and know that the Lord has set apart His faithful servant (you) for Himself; the Lord hears when you call Him.[vi] He will move you from victory to victory. Though you might fall, the Lord will pick you up. Though you might feel defeated, He will bring you to fullness. It's time to surrender. Read the prayer below as an example but ask The Holy Spirit to help you surrender your life over to Him. You can follow the prayer but allow The Holy Spirit to interject His voice. Allow your words to flow with His Spirit. Give your spirit room to surrender to the leading of The Holy Spirit. Then sign and date the page.

Remember this day is your spiritual funeral from your old life. And your rebirth into eternity with Love. Eternity with God! He's your commander in Chief now. ☺

My Father in heaven,

I come before you to confess I've made plenty of mistakes. I admit I am a sinner. I'm tired of doing things my way. I need you, Father. I surrender to you. Teach me to do things your way. I chose today to turn from my ways. I invite you into my life to be my Lord and my Savior. Heavenly Father fill the emptiness inside of me with your Holy Spirit. Father, bring peace where I have confusion. Bring joy where I have sadness. Fill me with your hope. By the blood of Jesus Christ that was shed on the cross, I confess, I am now being made whole, healed, and delivered. Because of His resurrection, I am made righteous. I declare that I am born again. Dead to my sins and alive in Jesus Christ from this day forward!

In the precious name of Jesus Christ, my life is sealed for Him, Amen!

_____   _____
Sign your name   Date

CONGRATULATIONS!!!!

You have died spiritually and are born again!!!!
Because of your testament of faith,
you and your household[vii] are saved![viii]

Below is a sample of the copyright-protected "New Spiritual Birth Certificate of Authenticity©" that awaits you.[ix] Just send an email to Saved@minister.com with "Born Again" as the subject line. Include a short testimony. Who were you and what prompted you to be saved? All of heaven rejoices with you, and so do I!

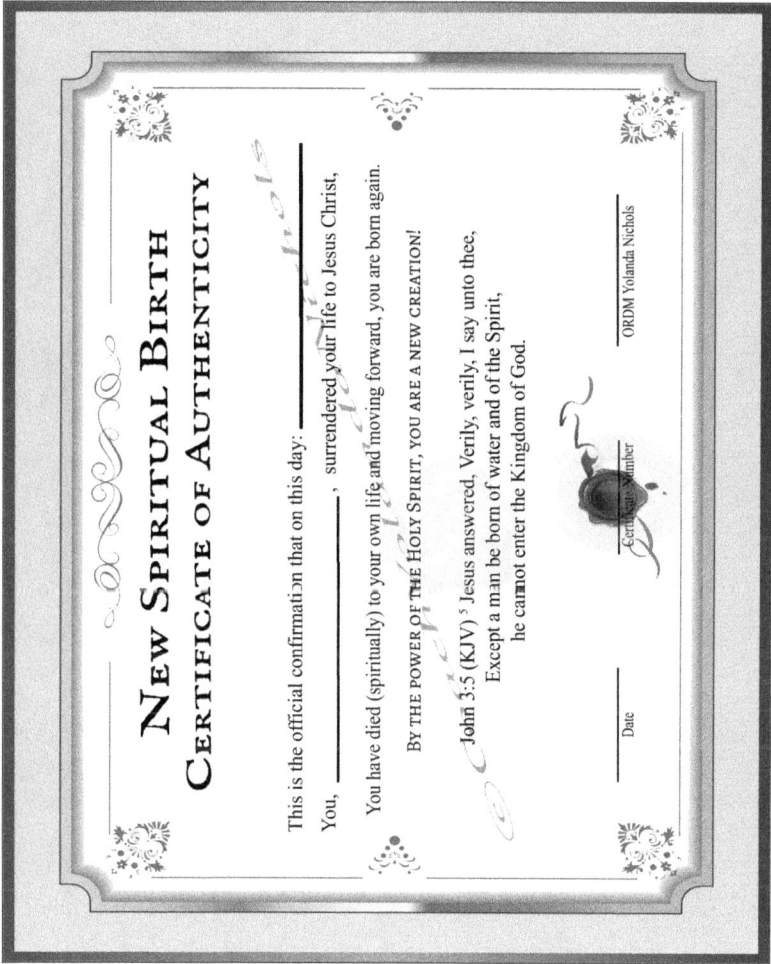

New Spiritual Birth Certificate of Authenticity

This is the official confirmation that on this day: _____

You, _____, surrendered your life to Jesus Christ,

You have died (spiritually) to your own life and moving forward, you are born again.

By the power of the Holy Spirit, you are a new creation!

John 3:5 (KJV) [5] Jesus answered, Verily, verily, I say unto thee, Except a man be born of water and of the Spirit, he cannot enter the Kingdom of God.

_____
Date

_____
Certificate Number

_____
ORDM Yolanda Nichols

The "2f" of this book

"Stop! I'm pregnant! I'm pregnant!," I screamed as he threw me over a two-story balcony. Dangling on the handrail, I looked at his eyes and knew he had evil in his heart. I knew this man, my husband, was going to kill me. Yet, that did not stop me from staying with him. Even after he attempted to end me and my unborn child's life, I went back to him. I was a slave to the evil inside of him. I didn't know who or whose I was. My soul was lost in the belly of the beast.

To clarify, my first husband was a physical weapon. One of many puppets, the enemy of humankind, used to try to kill me multiple times and tried to destroy my loved ones. But the Love of God for His children always wins. God's will prevails.

Truth be told, my story had a heartbreaking beginning since birth. My stepfather sexually molested me as a young child. Ripping me of my innocence. During one of my mother's old alcoholic rants, she told me she rejected me in the womb and cursed my existence. She even said that my grandmother tried to get her to get an abortion. I had no real friends growing up because of the guilt, shame, and condemnation that I carried from the sexual, verbal, physical, and emotional abuse. I wore a mask so people couldn't see me, let alone get to know me. As a young adult, I experimented with every addiction possible to destroy myself. I was my own worst enemy. As an adult, the dependencies continued but morphed into an even more profound false sense of identity. I experimented with same-sex relationships and engaged in extramarital affairs. Ruining at least two marriages and scarring my current marriage.

I've been homeless, panhandling, beaten, a drunkard, a drug user, and tried to commit suicide at least 3 times. I was on the expressway to hell. More about my story will be revealed through the pages of this study.

Yes, truth be told, my beginning, as well as, my middle was riddled with despair and hopelessness. There were many years filled with tears and trauma. However, as scripture says, my ending will be powerful and full of good fruit to bear.[x] Some good fruit is love, joy, hope, freedom, and peace.

Within that peace, I found the voice of Yâhh, the Hebrew God! I discovered that through Him, I had power in my words! I saw God's power through my voice. **This book was written to testify of HE who sent me and give you hope.** These decree's, declarations, confessions, and agreements are tools to help you through, what could be, a difficult journey. No matter how your beginning or middle looks, your ending will be powerful!

You see, we have word power! We have the scriptural responsibility to carry forth dominion and authority in our words. We are the rightful heirs to the throne of a King, the King of Kings. We are powerful! Friends, we are mighty! There is a force behind your words. You also, can overcome what the enemy has plotted, planned, strategically analyzed, and organized to take you and your loved ones out. Use the power God, the true God, the God of the Hebrews, gave you to fight.

Decreeing, declaring, confessing, and agreeing is not magic, nor incantation, nor religious philosophy. It is a spiritual strategical battle plan for a mental, physical, emotional, financial, and spiritual war. The formula is in scripture. All we have to do is use our tools, our voice, our power to elevate from that rocky beginning.

What does it mean to make a "Decree"?

In it's purest form, it is to determine what the outcome is expected to be with an announcement. According to Bakers – Evangelical – Dictionary on-line's[xi] definition simply put means, I am warning you it has been decided.

When you make a decree, you are making a notification, you have decided. You have dictated. For example, I decree you will be blessed by this book. You are also speaking to your past, present, and future. You are setting a foundational notification. Genesis 1 teaches us that God "notified," He spoke. He decreed. He decided. He commanded and dictated, "let there be light." He, God teaches us the power of our words. Believe it or not, we carry a lot of might in our speech.

In other words, God teaches us to make decrees because He knows we carry His power. Therefore, we are responsible for deciding what happens in the world around us. He wants us to notify the world: "Hey world, listen up!" He wants us to take a stand and change our world. We are not gods, we are His stewards. We dictate for Him.

Let it be known in Heaven, earth, and hell, we are taking ownership of our words to make changes, break bondage's, set captives free, and to live out loud the life God has created for us. The existence He initially designed for us! He said we are to live an abundant life. A life that is complete, full, and overflows. There is nothing broken inside or outside of us. Likewise, nothing is missing.

In contrary, lack is defined as; "to be deficient or missing"[xii] The Lord tells us we are to be lacking nothing. It means no debt, no diseases, no chaos, no calamities, especially within our Spirit man, the part of us that is Godly. It is where we commune with Adonai. Let's look at what scripture tells us:

> ### 1 Corinthians 2:14-16 (TPT)
>
> [14]Someone living on an entirely human level rejects the revelations of God's Spirit, for they make no sense to him. He can't understand the revelations of the Spirit because they are only discovered by the illumination of the Spirit. [15] Those who live in the Spirit are able to carefully evaluate all things, and they are subject to the scrutiny of no one but God. [16] For Who has ever intimately known the mind of the Lord Yahweh well enough possess Christ's perceptions.

As you can see, the Spirit man provides the abundance from the relationship with Jesus Christ. Bounty in relationships. Yes, that means a healthy-loving marriage. A healthy-loving relationship with your children. A healthy-loving relationship with your in-laws. It means a healthy-loving accord within the Body of Christ. We have health, provision, safety, and security. We have precisely what we need in abundant life. We will create that abundant life when we take back our word power. When we decree. When we utter life! When we open our mouths to use our word power!

I am forewarning heaven, hell, and the world, this is what is going to happen! You have been served! You have been notified! Our maker has given us the power to speak, to inform, and decide the outcome of any event. We are co-laboring with Him. When we are connected to Him, He knows He can trust us with our words.

So speak! Decree! Bring forward the will of the Father. Speak His heart into existence. Speak His love. Release His notifications. Release His promises! Release His divinity! Release His goodness! Release His power through you!

What does it mean to make a "Declaration"?

When a King or a Queen writes a declaration, they are stating that a command will be enacted. It will be performed and or carried out without questioning the order. With the authority that they have the action will, without question, happen. We have a God-given authority.

LUKE 9:1
Declares our

Power
&
Authority

We have been commissioned to speak God's plan. When we verbalize a command, our God-given authority aligns with God's government, it will happen without a doubt! The seal takes place when we speak the mandate on behalf of Adonai. A seal is a Kingdom guarantee. A guarantee from the heart of the Father. Therefore, a declaration is a Stamp of a Kingdom Authority for an action to happen without questioning. Without any rebuttals. God said to make a declaration to change the world. He even instructed us to have an ear to hear the instructions of the Spirit; see Revelation 3:22. When we are connected with The Holy Spirit, we command the declarations out of the Spirit of Yâhh. We don't randomly declare, we declare His heart. We proclaim His will. We proclaim His instructions.

The oneness with God allows us to know precisely what declarations need to be made. It is His Spirit that uses our mouth to speak His will. We are the yielded vessels, meaning we volunteer to be used by Him for the betterment of everyone. It is not magic. It is guaranteeing God's will, will happen.

To be sure, in Revelation 3:22, Abba tells us to listen to and respond to His plea. Please note, it is not John speaking but The Holy Spirit speaking to the Ekklesia[xiii] (the called ones/ the church). The Spirit will guide us into making Kingdom declarations. These declarations will transform us, our family, and the people around us. Through the declarations, we can speak God's will over any situation we want to change, and we will see His hand manifest. We will see His will be done! Especially when we have scripture to back it up. This is not an incantation or witchcraft but a surrendering to the Spirit's leading in absolute obedience. Hear the Spirit and speak the Spirit. For this, you have to be empty of you and full of His Word.

What does it mean to make a "Confession"?

According to Merriam-Webster's definition of confession[xiv], we are confessing with a natural oral acknowledgment of a common creed. In other words, we are acknowledging the Word of Adonai and impregnating it to our soul. Our soul[xv] is essentially our mind, emotions, and will. It is the part of us that makes us human.

Our mind is like a computer chip but inside our brain. Our brain is the physical matter of our minds. Our mind stores memories, reasoning, logic, purpose, and even our fears. It is what propels us to push forward. At times, to retreat. It is the place inside of us that tells the brain to produce serotonin. An essential ingredient for our survival. Too much or too little serotonin can have an impact on our emotions.

Our emotions are the cognitive results of our minds. We experience them physically. There's a wide range of emotions, and we can experience two or three at a time.

Psalm 36:7 (NIV)

[7]How priceless is your unfailing love, O God! People take refuge in the shadow of your wings.

For example, some people on the Autism spectrum can experience them all at once. Some emotions are anger, fear, hatred, rejection, happiness, gratitude, joy, and love. God gave us feelings because He is an emotional being. There are lots of scriptures that validate He is an emotional being. Still, let's look at just one example for Love (an emotion). To love someone is to give them free will. God has blessed us with free will because of the love He has for us. He doesn't want robots. He wants children who chose to love Him out of their free will.

Now a quick definition of our will is; our character or the choices we make. It is who we are. Yet, our freedom does not mean we get to do whatever we want. We have a responsibility. Especially as believers of the One True God. We can't just do whatever we want.

> Galatians 5:13 (AMP)
>
> [13]For you, my brothers, were called to freedom; only do not let your freedom become an opportunity for the sinful nature (worldliness, selfishness), but through love serve and seek the best for one another.

So, why do we need to make confessions? We need to make confessions because we have been programmed into believing the world and their interpretation of who we are. We, for a long time, have accepted outside sources for an internal belief. Those are lies that bind us.

Case in point, I believed I was doomed to be abused, mistreated, neglected, and rejected for my entire life. I had a victim mentality. However, that is a lie from the pit of hell. Now, I make daily confessions of who God says I am in Him. He calls me blessed, chosen, cherished, treasured, and loved. Just to name a few. <wink>

Given that we have believed lies for a long time, we need to make life-changing confessions. We need to heal our spirit and soul: which is the mind, emotions, and will. When we make confessions, we are being reconstructed to who He says we are.

What does it mean to "Agree"?

When we two or three agree, nothing can be impossible. That is the promise of God. When you, The Holy Spirit, and I come into an agreement under the oath of Matthew 18:19-20, in honor of God, He comes right in and honors the request. It is powerful when two or three come into agreement. That is the heart of God. Unity and agreements between His children. No parent wants to see their children bickering and fighting. It is even more powerful when we come into agreement with His Word. When we agree, in love and faith.

Matthew 18:19-20 (TPT)

[19]Again, I give you an eternal truth: If two of you agree to ask God for something in a symphony of prayer, my heavenly Father will do it for you. [20] For wherever two or three come together in honor of my name, I am right there with them!

Furthermore, Merriam-Webster's dictionary, in short, states it is to concede[xvi]. It means we give up what we believe to be the truth, for what Adonai says is truth. It means we don't rely on our five senses; sound, taste, touch, sight, and smell. We trust His Word. His, Elohim's, Word is infallible. It means it can not be broken, undone, unloosed,[xvii] and or destroyed. The Word of Elohim is unbreakable. There's absolutely nothing you can do to break His Word. You are not that powerful so relax, He's got you! His Word says so.

Let's look at an example. When we feel sick, lonely, tired, unworthy, unloved, unappreciated, rejected, or whatever negative feeling we have, we don't agree with it. That's when we take out our Bibles and do thorough scripture research. Thus the creation of this book. We want to get out of our minds. What does He want us to believe and think? For a quick study, see 1 Peter 4.

Besides, we must ask, what does Adonai say about your negative feelings? What does His Word say about your current situation? What does He say about your thoughts, family, friends, neighborhood, ministry, business, and or your employment? What does God say about your emotional health? Where do you need tweaking in your thoughts?

For this purpose, when we agree with Abba, we reroute our brainwaves from our thinking and into His thinking. We concede our thoughts. After all, His thoughts are much better. Let us come into agreement with His Word. Let us agree with Him.

A Decree says:

I am warning you this will happen!

You have been served with a

legislative warrant!

A Declaration says:

I have an official seal to make the

warrant happen!

The warrant is being executed.

A Confession says:

I am making a creed of the truth. I confess His Word to be accurate.

To Agree with means to concede.

Not what I want but what He wants.

Not my will but His.

I agree God is right.

Are you ready?

Are you ready to silence the lies of the enemy and learn how to apply God's truth to them? Are you ready to begin making decrees, declarations, confessions, and agreements? Are you ready to change the world you live in? Are you ready to change your marriage so that it can bring honor and glory to God? Are you ready to shape your children's future? Are you ready to see a shift in your children-in-love? Are you ready to shift your city? Are you ready to see a change in your government? Are you ready to position your life for the blessings of the Lord Jesus Christ to flow to you and through you? Are you ready to speak life into your atmosphere? Are you ready to take your power back? Are you ready for God to use you?

Granted, there are many books on decrees and declarations. In no way am I ever stating this bible study is the end all and be all to decreeing and declaring. Allow this book to be another tool in your toolbox. The more tools you have, the more successful you will be. Your success will be evident with every victory scar. Wear your victory scars proudly. Our victory scars point to One God, Yâhh, the God of Abraham, Isaac, Moses, Joshua, Jacob, Paul, Peter, and Mary. The God who gives you and me breath to live. The God that has been with you every day of your life.

Above all, my prayer for you is that you use every tool at your disposal. Every tool turns into a weapon. Every weapon adds to your arsenal. With enough of an arsenal, you are guaranteed a victorious battle. Remember, you win in the end, as God has declared it, but we are to engage in the war. We are to face the enemy of our soul with our tools in place. No soldier goes to battle without their weapons or equipment. So, learn to engage in defense and offense in this spiritual battle fully equipped.

With these powerful tools, decrees, declarations, confessions, and agreements, you will change your future and change the future of your loved ones. You can change the future of everyone, you know. Trust the process! Because it is a process! Stick with it! The Lord will take you from one victory to the next. He wants to use your voice to command the earth and for it to be subdued.[xviii]

Despite that, we are not gods, and we do not speak witchcraft. We are commanded to subdue the earth. That is what we are doing in this Bible study. We are taking dominion over what the enemy thinks he has seized from us. Remember you, are victorious, so call his bluff! Always keep that in the forefront when you want to quit. Because you will want to. Remember, you are already victorious! You are taking ownership back and obeying Abba's instructions to subdue the earth. Your Heavenly Father is the King of Kings, and He has commanded you to make decrees, declarations, confessions, and agreements with your future, today!

Furthermore, share with everyone you know the blessings of this book. Share with them the power of words that God has given you. Speak Life to everyone you know and every situation in your life. You can change everything going on in your life. The Lord, Abba, has given you the power to do so! So share with people. Share with them the knowledge you have gained. Share with them how to transform their atmosphere. Share with them how they can reshape their children's and grandchildren's children's future. For generations to come.

When we share what we have received, we position ourselves for even more blessings from the Lord-Abba. He loves you so much, and He is cheering for you. He wants to see you prosper, and He wants to see you help others prosper. You are His changing agent. You are His hands, His feet, His mouth, His eyes, and, more importantly, His heart. He will use a willing and yielded vessel. Are you ready to be the willing and yielded vessel?

Moreover, when the Lord-Abba sees you are a willing and yielded vessel who continuously gives out, guess what... He gives you more. He pours more into your cup when you have emptied it for others. He is watching you. He knows your heart. He knows you want to share the blessings with others, so be bold, be courageous, and be giving. Share!

Even further, you bring a smile on His face when you are obedient. Speak, decree, declare, confess, and agree. Change what needs to be changed. Change your atmosphere. Change your course and that of your loved ones. Remember, you are His vessel. He is counting on you. He wants you to open your mouth and speak positive-life giving commands. Speak! Open your mouth and use your word power to release His will!

Exhortation & Activation

I decree, declare, confess, and agree that you carry the wisdom of Jesus Christ. So rest knowing you have His wisdom.[xix]

I decree, declare, confess, and agree that you have the right mind of Jesus Christ that you think and act like Jesus Christ. His mind is your mind. So rest knowing you think as Christ thinks.[xx]

I decree, declare, confess, and agree that your mind is expanding to grasp the knowledge that Jesus Christ is downloading to you as you read this book. He opens your mind to new revelations. So, receive it![xxi]

I decree, declare, confess, and agree that God's angels are surrounding you right now and protecting you from confusion, doubt, and fear. You are now entering the presence of the Lord Jesus Christ.[xxii]

I command the spirits of doubt, fear, confusion, untrust, unforgiveness, bitterness, resentfulness, apathy, conformity, lies, and deceit to leave your atmosphere now. In the name of Yeshua HaMashiach! Amen![xxiii]

I replace the emptiness of these evil spirits with the True Spirit of Wisdom, confidence, security, protection, trust, forgiveness, humbleness, boldness, clarity, certainty, love, and truthfulness of the true Holy Spirit.[xxiv]

I loosen your mind to the mind of Jesus Christ. Holy Spirit fill every space with your presence. In the precious cherished name of Jesus Christ, I seal this prayer in your spirit, heart, mind, and soul. I decree, declare, confess, and agree that you are whole, healed, and delivered. Amen!

Abba, I pray the Kabod of Jesus Christ to fall in and through your children. Meet them where they are. Move them to where you want them to go. Let them feel you in every prayer, decree, declaration, confession, agreement, and activation.

Father, restore them to your will. May nothing be broken, and may nothing be missing in them. Restore their soul and their spirit. Only you, Abba, can do the surgery needed in their hearts. Only you transform, redeem, and purify. So, we thank you for finishing the work you are doing, and we say yes to your every command. We say yes to your process. Father, I, invite you to dwell in this study. May your will be done.

Abba, we bless, honor, worship, adore, cherish, and love you. We thank you for your goodness, mercy, faithfulness, and your love. Only you are Holy, worthy, kind, faithful, and loving. Father, in the precious name of Jesus Christ, I pray, Amen! ♥

21 Days of change to a new you

In 1960, cosmetic surgeon Maxwell Maltz wrote a book entitled, Psycho-Cybernetics[xxv]. In that book, he describes how people that have undergone plastic surgeries and amputations take about 21 days to get used to their new looks. He also noticed that the same was true about changes in his life, and thus the idea was born of "21 days to form a new habit."

Since then, many other scientists, writers, motivational speakers, coaches, and or spiritual leaders (including Christians) have backed up his theory that it takes a minimum of 21 days for these changes to settle into our minds. In other words, for real transformation to manifest[xxvi]. Its fruit will be evident in 21 days.

On that theory, my challenge to you is to go through the 21 lies one day at a time. Again, first, skim the book to see what the material consists of. Then read each day and let it seep in. As you do the study, allow the transformation power of God to work in you. He alone will transform you into His divine purpose because He created you with a plan and purpose: see Jeremiah 29:11.

Furthermore, you will experience resistance. Again, you might want to quit. You might want to cry in the process. All those emotions and feelings are perfectly normal. You are collaborating with God to change the way you think. You are washing your brain, removing the muck, and replacing it with the clarity of Jesus Christ. Just remember, you are dying to who you were or who you thought you were to become who God wants you to be. Dying is a process, you are killing your old self so that you can become who, He says you are! Your true identity! Abba's true son and daughter. Co-heirs to the Heavenly Throne by Christ, Jesus.

With that in mind, give yourself permission to grieve and feel the spiritual resistance. While publishing this book, I experienced resistance. I experienced many challenges, including but not limited to, breaking my leg. I was on bed rest for almost a year. Eventually, the injury developed into Complex Regional Pain Syndrome, meaning total and permanent nerve damage.

At times my foot and my total body hurt so bad I did not want to write. There were days I could not even get out of bed. Some days I did not even want to open my Bible. Praying and worshiping were the farthest thing on my mind. At times, showering was the most significant achievement. I postponed finishing the book because I did not feel worthy. There were many times I quit writing.

Furthermore, this book took almost 5 years to write. With 4 different shifts happening within the text. Yet, I pushed through it because it is not about me! This book is inspired by The Holy Spirit. Like our Biblical heroes, I had to be obedient. I had to make a choice. Obey Yâhh (true God) or obey the enemy of my soul. Whose voice would I listen to? In disobedience, the Lord will allow things to happen to make us uncomfortable because He cares about us. His discipline is for our sake. So, I put myself aside and obeyed Yâhh. ☺

Foundationally, Yâhh, the one true God, is outside the lies of the enemy. Let Him breakthrough to you. Jesus is waiting for you to let Him through. Don't focus on what the enemy of humankind is doing. Instead, focus on what Yeshua HaMashiach is doing. Ask Him, "Jesus, what am I what am I being taught?" Better yet, ask yourself, "What is God training me for?" Is He pruning, building, or repairing?

With that in mind, let's agree, **warfare is real!** It is physical, spiritual, emotional, financial, and intellectual war. As I shared in my story, and the enemy does not play fair, the enemy of our soul truly hates us. He wants to destroy us.

> John 10:10 (AMP)
>
> [10]The thief comes only in order to steal kill and destroy. I came that they may have and enjoy life, and have it in abundance [to the full, till it overflows]

In God's word, John 10:10, it clearly states the enemy of humanity is ONLY, did you catch that ONLY here to kill, steal, and destroy us! Still, fear not, God has made us victorious.

Stop before moving forward!

Before diving into the pages, prepare your heart and your mind. Find a quiet place to read the scriptures in the chapter. Meditate on them, read the prayers, and allow the person of The Holy Spirit to love you. Marinate on the scriptures. Let them seep into your being. Season your life with His Word. Spice up your thoughts and your actions based on His promptings.

As you study the Word, you will experience a change in you. Also, people will begin to notice. Yet, never expect perfection from yourself or anyone else. Always walk-in grace and humility. When people are rude or disrespectful to you as you walk through this process, remember it is a condition of their heart, not yours. Don't take the bait and walk in forgiveness. Forgive them. Give yourself and others grace as you heal.

As you press forward, each day will guide you to a breakthrough. Meaning there will be a shift in your thinking. Each breakthrough will be painful, but oh so worth it. This pain (mostly emotional) will bring you freedom. Marinate in this newfound freedom that each day brings. Marinate in the essence of God. In His essence, you will find freedom, deliverance, safety, security, love, peace, joy, and happiness. Everything you need to shift the world around you!

As you trust the Lord, you will see His hand manifest in your life. You will see His promises delivered to you and yours. You will see He blesses you because He wants to bless you. Not because you have earned it but just because He wants to bless you.

Always remember He is a good, loving, kind, merciful, faithful, trustworthy, grateful, and benevolent Daddy! He wants to bless you in every sense of the word. He promised Abram abundant blessings: see Genesis 17, and those promises fall on you and yours because we are Abram's descendants.[xxvii]

Galatians 3:16 (TPT)

[16]Remember the royal proclamation God spoke over Abraham and to Abraham's child? God said that His promises were made to pass on to Abraham's "child" not children. And who is this "child?? It's the Son of promise, Jesus, the Messiah!

Through Jesus Christ, we became the chosen heirs! Let us walk, talk, and straighten-up because our Savior has given us the Kingdom. We are Royalty! No matter what it looks like right now to you or to others, YOU ARE ROYALTY! Dust off your crown and speak your authority! Use your voice! Use your God-given word power!

♥ *Ready to begin? Let's do this! I'm with you all the way & most importantly Abba is with you!* ♥

Section Two: Let's Begin Our Study!

For where two or three are gathered together in
My name, I am there in the midst of them.

Matthew 18:20 (NKJV

Day One: Ambiguity & Doubt

The lies we sometimes believe:

The enemy plants ambiguity and doubt in our minds. We doubt if we are genuinely saved. We doubt if we are good enough. We doubt because we don't have all the answers. We doubt because we've lost interest in the things that should matter the most. We doubt Jesus Christ. There is ambiguity or doubt in our faith and our walk with Jesus Christ.

The truth that sets us free:

Matthew 11:3-5 (HCSB)

[3]and asked Him, "Are you the One who is to come, or should we expect someone else?"

[4]Jesus replied to them, "Go and report to John what you hear and see: [5] the blind see, the lame walk, those with skin diseases are healed, the deaf hear, the dead are raised, and the poor are told the good news.

Reconciling the lie with the truth:

There is true faith in those who are in Jesus Christ. Simple! We have to agree that we will not have any ambiguity or doubt in our hearts. Either we believe scripture or we don't. Believing in scripture gives us hope, freedom, assurance, and a plethora of blessings.

Time to Decree, Declare, Confess, and Agree:

I decree, declare, confess, and agree that Jesus Christ died in the flesh, defeated death, He is the King of Kings and Lord of Lords. I decree, declare, confess, and agree that my faith is true because of the sacrifice of Jesus Christ. I decree that when the enemy plants doubt or ambiguity, I will shout a resounding joy because I am saved, healed, delivered, and made whole. There is nothing inside of me that is missing or has broken pieces. I confess there is true faith in me because of the Blood of Jesus Christ that was shed at the cross on Calvary.

I agree with Elohim when He says my faith is rooted and grounded in His love. His love is the fluid coursing through my veins. He is my fixed foundation.

I decree, declare, confess, and agree that doubt has no place inside of me. My soul, which is my spirit, mind, will, and emotions are rooted and grounded in His love and His Word. He has the final authority and say in my life.

Day One: Establishing Your Faith

We want to be rooted and grounded in love. Because Love is what will transform us from the darkness into the light. Jesus Christ is love: see 1 John 4:8, so we must first understand who Jesus Christ is. Take out your Bible and look up these scriptures. Take the time to read them. Let them sift in your thoughts. What do they say to you? Write down your thoughts as you read the scriptures. Where is your heart? Ask yourself, who is Jesus Christ in each scripture? Then write out your personal confession of the Word.

1 Peter 1:20, John 1:1-13, Matthew 3:17, John 8:12, 1 John 2:1

Day Two: Bad Witness

The lies we sometimes believe:

I can't be angry at God! The anger causes me to doubt my salvation, and therefore I can't evangelize. If I can't evangelize, I can't be a good witness. If I am not a good witness, I need more ministry training. I am a lousy witness. I need to always be happy. People need to see or think that my life is perfect.

The truth that sets us free:

Hebrews 12:2 (NIV)
2fixing our eyes on Jesus, the pioneer, and perfecter of faith. For the joy set before him, He endured the cross, scorning its shame, and sat down at the right hand of the throne of God.

Replacing the lie with the truth:

When Jesus Christ is our fixed end goal, our focal point, we can trust that just as He completed His race in perfection, so shall we. We witness to others by how we live our life. It's sometimes a perfect mess, but that highlights, even more, our dependence on Him. The true perfector of our lives. He is the one that moves us, changes us, and eventually transforms us. He is the one that gives us words to say to the lost[xxviii]. He is the one who moves through us and creates a catalyst for change. Let us fix our eyes on the one true love- Jesus Christ.

Time to Decree, Declare, Confess, and Agree:

Glorious Abba, I repent from ever being angry at you. You are gentle and humble. Abba, I repent from any doubt and even doubting my salvation. I repent from not healthily acknowledging my emotions. You gave us righteous anger. Unrighteous anger is a product of the enemy of humankind working his schemes in my mind. I repent Father!

Abba, I rest, knowing you have saved me! Abba, I decree, declare, confess, and agree, I am a good witness everywhere I go. You are the ministry trainer. You are the perfecter of my walk. You are my road-map. I decree, declare, confess, and agree that I fix my eyes on you, Jesus Christ. Thank you, Abba, for loving me, for teaching me, for convicting me, and for being my pioneer. You are worthy! You are Holy! We bless you! In Jesus Christ's name, I pray, Amen!

Day Two: Confirm Your Foundation

We've studied who Jesus Christ was. We learned some of His attributes. Now let's look at what He did. As you read these verses, listen for His voice. What is He trying to tell you through the verses? You will manifest good witnessing when you've confirmed your foundation is Jesus Christ and Him alone. He is our solid rock.

1 Corinthians 15:3, Revelation 1:18, John 8:36, 1 Peter 3:21-22, 2 Corinthians 5:18

_____

_____

_____

_____

_____

_____

_____

_____

_____

_____

_____

_____

Day Three: Death

The lies we sometimes believe:

I have a fear of death. Will this illness kill me? Will one of my loved ones get hurt or killed? What if I die without repenting? What will happen to my loved ones if I die? What if I decree, declare, confess, and agree, and nothing changes, and my loved one dies?

The truth that sets us free:

John 3:16 (TPT)

[16]For this is how much God loved the world-He gave His one and only, unique Son as a gift. So now everyone who believes in Him will never perish but experience everlasting life.

Replacing the lie with the truth:

Death in the natural is but a beginning in the eternal. For the obedient believer, we will experience everlasting life before the presence of the One true God. For the disobedient believer, it will all depend on the status of their heart. Do you have an unrepentant heart? For a hardened heart and or unbeliever, unfortunately, they will experience eternal life in Sheol. More about that later in the book.

To be clear, the Lord cannot move in an unrepentant heart, believer, or not. Meaning, He will never violate a person's will. However, He will allow the dogs of heaven, aka angels of destruction,[xxix] to invade a person until they are convicted. Until there is a heart change. Also, sometimes a person's healing is graduating to heaven. Meaning they die in the natural but live eternally before the King.

That is why we need to stand in the gap and use our words wisely. Remember, we are speaking His will out of the connection we have with Him. If our motives and heart are pure, He will move in any situation according to His will.

Time to Decree, Declare, Confess, and Agree:

I decree, declare, confess, and agree that Jesus Christ is the Son of God. I decree, declare, confess, and agree, I am a child of God! I decree, declare, confess, and agree by faith, that I and my loved ones[xxx] will experience eternal life because we believe in Jesus Christ. No weapon formed against me or mine shall prosper, including untimely death. I rebuke the spirit of premature death in my life and the lives of my loved ones. We have been washed by the Blood of the Lamb. We will experience everlasting life.

Abba, we offer the sacrifice of faith, you have overcome the world. We receive by grace the knowledge that you have destroyed death. We agree it is your love that moves us to repentance from our sinful nature.[xxxi] We rest knowing you protect us. Thank you, Father! Thank you for who you are! You are divine and eternal! In the glorified name of Jesus Christ, I pray, Amen!

Day Three: Eternal Peaceful Life

Jesus Christ is currently seated at the right hand of Yâhh. He broke the curse of death when He sacrificed His life for us. We do not have to fear death. We can learn to embrace it as believers because He gives us eternal life. His reparation for our sins created a bridge for us to be connected with Father God. As well as for us to have everlasting life. An eternal life. All we have to do is rest in Him. He will walk us through the process of reaching the end goal; salvation, sanctification, justification, purification, and eventually glorification. Through Jesus Christ, we have eternal life. Let us be grateful for His goodness!

> ## Mark 16:19 (HCSB)
>
> [19]Then after speaking to them, the Lord Jesus was taken up into heaven and sat down at the right hand of God.

When we remember the goodness of YHWH, we can walk out our fear of death. Remember, He has destroyed death once and for all. We don't have to fear death. Our bodies might break down, but our last breath will bring us into our first eternal breath.

Besides, as long as our loved ones are protected because we cover them in prayers, and Jesus Christ prays[xxxii] for them, we do not have to fear if and when something attacks them. Remember, Jesus Christ is constantly interceding for us because the enemy is bombarding with accusations. They have the best security ever. Our loved ones have the best doctor, healer, and comforter.

Further, when we are in constant prayer, (prayer is a conversation with God), we are intimate with Jesus Christ. He is the one who moves us to Holy repentance. Guilt, shame, and condemnation are not from His heart. Any of those negative feelings are from the enemy of humankind. Holy conviction is from our Father.

To add, as we stay in the Presence of Jesus Christ, we will experience a heart transformation. This heart transformation is spiritual surgery. The spiritual surgery is done in and through us. So don't fear my friend because our final glory days are coming when we stand before the presence of Yâhh.

For day three, write a thank you letter to God. Thank Him for protecting you and your loved ones. Thank Him for healing you and your loved ones. Thank Him for eternal life. Thank Him for the gift of repentance.

As a matter of fact, did you know that repentance is a gift?[xxxiii] He could easily take us out with His wrath. Just like He did the Egyptians who tried to cross the Jordan river, or when someone was disobedient, or when the Children of Israel had idols.

Beloveds, despite our actions, His wrath is not like a human's wrath. His wrath is divine. It is justified. It is Holy wrath. Much like when our parents tell us not to touch the stove because it's hot. Some children don't touch the stove while others test their boundaries. Those children inevitably get burned. That is precisely how God's wrath is! His wrath is to protect us. It is Holy indignation. It is an emotional expression of His love for us. "Beware my children! Beware!"[xxxiv]

Now take some time to thank Him for withholding His wrath. Thank Him and praise Him. Remember His goodness. Remember His kindness. Remember His gentleness. Thank Him! Remember, He spared you from His wrath. Remember that as a saved child, you now have an eternal peaceful life. If you need more space, just use a blank paper.

_____

_____

_____

_____

_____

_____

_____

_____

_____

Day Four: The Enemy of Humankind

The lies we sometimes believe:

The devil does not exist. If he does live, he has my power and authority. The devil was conjured up to manipulate the masses.

The truth that sets us free:

The fall of Lucifer.
Luke 10:18 (TPT)
18Jesus replied, "While you were ministering, I watched satan topple until he fell suddenly from heaven like lightning to the ground.

Jesus conquers satan
Colossians 2:15 (AMP)
15When He had disarmed the rulers and authorities [those supernatural forces of evil operating against us], He made a public example of them [exhibiting them as captives in His triumphal procession], having triumphed over them through the cross.

Jesus has final authority
Ephesians 1:21 (TPT)
21And now, He is exalted as first above every ruler, authority, government, and realm of power in existence! He is gloriously enthroned over every name that is ever praised, not only in this age, but in the age that is coming!

Replacing the lie with the truth:

Since we believe wholeheartedly in Jesus Christ, we have to recognize his enemy. Who happens to be the enemy of humankind. Our mortal enemy, the devil. So yes, my friend, there is a devil, and he is on the prowl to kill, steal, and destroy everything you have and everything you love.

The truth is, satan,[xxxv] the devil,[xxxvi] who was named Lucifer[xxxvii] upon his creation, fell from heaven, renamed,[xxxviii] lives and breathes today. Because he is alive, we are to be alert and have a sober mind. If we are not on our guard, he will bind our minds from understanding the true gospel of Jesus Christ. He, the devil prowls like a roaring lion looking for whom to devour.[xxxix]

To clarify, he, Lucifer, now known satan or the devil, fell from heaven because "He did not want to do what he was created to do."[xl] Though he was created with "riches and honor"[xli] and was the highest ranking archangel, he rebelled against His creator. He wanted and still wants to be God. Don't get confused; he is the god[xlii] of this world but not the true God. He cannot create life. He merely mimics.

Consequently, Jesus Christ conquers the power of satan[xliii]. He, Jesus Christ, our Messiah, defeated satan by being God made flesh, resisting temptation, proclaiming the good news, dying, and resurrecting on the 3rd day. By His death and resurrection, He made a public spectacle of satan. Took back his authority and dismantled it. Giving Him, Christ, the final jurisdiction overall. His sacrifice has the final say, and now He works through us. Thus the creation of this book. You don't have to fear the enemy of your soul, he is defeated!

Time to Decree, Declare, Confess, and Agree:

Kyrios (Kü'-rē-os) (supremacy), I decree, declare, confess, and agree that you are the King of Kings, the Lord of Lords, the Alpha and the Omega. There is no god above you.

Kyrios, I decree, declare, confess, and agree that the enemy of humankind does exist. Still, he has no power over me or mine. For your word says in Luke 10:19 that you have given us authority over the power of the enemy of humankind. I decree, declare, confess, and agree with your Word that says nothing shall harm us. No weapon he forms shall prosper.

As we resist him, he has to flee. By your Word, we have power over the works of the enemy of your soul As the days get darker, your Light shines brighter in us and through us. Thank you, Kyrios, for warning us of this serpent. Thank you for protecting us. You are the Supreme Lord, the Master, the Kyrios! In Jesus Christ's name, I pray, Amen!

Day Four: Jesus Christ The Friend of Man

We know that the enemy of humankind is roaming around like a caged lion.[xliv] He's looking for an opportunity to devour you and yours. All he wants to do is kill, steal, and destroy everything in you and around you. He's not a passive enemy. No, he is an active ferocious beast waiting to eat its prey. He's full of anger, vengeance, and hatred. There's nothing in him that's true. Nothing in him is pure. He is a liar, and spews lies. He will devour you and yours if you do not go on the offense. If you believe his lies, you are a slave to him and his every whim. Like, I was, in my childhood, as a young adult, and even in some parts of my adult years. Until I accepted and surrendered my life over to Yeshua HaMashiach, our Redeemer.

Still, some people deny the existence of the beast. In fact, he's okay with that. He wants people (believers or not) to doubt his existence. Because if he can get you to question his presence, then he has his gnarly fangs on you and yours. You can't escape the golden cage he has you in if you deny his existence. My friends, the devil exists! The only way to see his cage is to accept Jesus Christ as your personal Lord and Savior. Only then can you see his fangs in your life.

So, where is Jesus Christ if the enemy is active and alive? Christ, Himself, is vibrant and alive! He wages war on the enemy of humankind for God's children. Whether they believe in the one true God or not. He wages war for everyone; believer and non-believer.

Let's look over some scriptures that prove Jesus Christ is actively living.

1. Jesus Christ is actively praying for us, see; Hebrews 7:25, Romans 8:34, 1 John 2:1

2. Jesus Christ is actively working as second in command in the spiritual war for us, see; Matthew 28:18-20, Acts 2:36, Ephesians 1:20-23

3. Jesus Christ is equipping us with spiritual tools, see; Acts 2:46-47, Acts 2:32-33, Galatians 1:11-12

4. Jesus Christ is preparing a palace for each one of us, see; John 14:2-3, Colossians 1:12, Matthew 25:34

Furthermore, He, Christ Jesus, works through us, believers. He uses you and me to get through to this world. The moment you were saved, the Lord gave you a job. You became His Ambassador on earth. You are expected to do your assignment, which is His will.

Do not be like the enemy of humankind and not carry out what you were created to do. Do not rebel against God by being a child of disobedience. Disobedience will only unleash the dogs of heaven. Instead, be like Jesus Christ and humble yourself in obedience. Carry out your job assignment.

For your study time, part 1, is to write down what is stopping you from believing that the enemy of humankind exists. What is the block in your mind that is unable to comprehend that we have a spiritual enemy? As always, ask The Holy Spirit to help you with this process. Ask Him to lift the veil that is in your eyes.

For part 2, let's look at what scripture has to say about the enemy of humankind. Write down your thoughts as you read the scriptures. What do you feel, hear, and see? It is when we face the enemy that we can see him and eventually overcome him. As always, pray and stay connected with The Holy Spirit. As you go through this process, ask Jesus Christ to help you. Remember, He is praying for you.

Isaiah 14:12-15

_____

_____

_____

_____

_____

_____

Ezekiel 28:12-19

_____

_____

_____

_____

_____

Revelation 12:7-12

_____

_____

_____

_____

_____

Matthew 4:1-11

_____

_____

_____

_____

_____

James 4:7

_____

_____

_____

_____

_____

According to Merriam-Webster,
the definition of a **breakthrough** is;

1. Warfare: an offensive military assault that penetrates and carries beyond a defensive line.

2. : an act or instance of moving through or beyond an obstacle

3. a: a sudden advance especially in knowledge or technique
   b: **a person's first notable success**

► When you can see the enemy's tactics you can breakthrough his plans. ◄

Day Five: Evil

The lies we sometimes believe:

No matter how much I try, bad things will always happen. This world is full of evil. I deserved to be punished. People are so evil.

The truth that sets us free:

1 Peter 3:9 (AMP)

[9]and never return evil for evil or insult for insult [avoid scolding, berating, and any kind of abuse], but on the contrary, give a blessing [pray for one another's well-being, contentment, and protection]; for you have been called for this very purpose, that you might inherit a blessing [from God that brings well being, happiness, and protection].

Replacing the lie with the truth:

When the enemy is throwing his best punches, dig your toes in God's word, root yourself in His promises, and rest. Let Christ do the fighting for you. Stand on His Word, especially the red letters.

Similarly, show compassion to those who are not in accord with you. Let your love speak louder than your need to be right. Guard your tongue and always speak heavenly things. Speak the goodness of God. Speak His will over everyone and everything around you. If you see evil, ask The Holy Spirit, what He wants you to do about it. It might be to write a book. <wink>

Time to Decree, Declare, Confess, and Agree:

Adonai, our eyes, ears, and heart betray us, but you do not. I decree, declare, confess, and agree that YOUR Word that is oozing with Love is the ultimate authority. I decree, declare, confess, and agree that you will never betray us. I pray blessings over all who call themselves my enemies. I decree my tongue speaks only of your goodness, your kindness, and of your Holiness! I speak only of your love. I decree that you are my protection, I shall not fear the evil around me. You are the Supreme Ruler overall. Thank you, Adonai! Thank you! All honor and all glory to You, Adonai! In Jesus Christ name, I pray, Amen

2nd Corinthians 4:4 (TPT)
4for their minds have been blinded by the god of this age, leaving them in unbelief. Their blindness keeps them from seeing the dayspring light of the wonderful news of the glory of Jesus Christ, who is the divine image of God.

Day Five: The Goodness of God

Let's study some verses that talk about the goodness of God. As you read the verses, ask Him to speak to your heart. Write down what you hear Him saying to your heart about His heart. You will begin to see the goodness around you when you understand His goodness.

Psalm 34:8 (NIV) ⁸Taste and see that the Lord is good; blessed is the one who takes refuge in Him.

_____

_____

_____

_____

James 1:17 (AMP) ¹⁷Every good thing given and every perfect gift is from above; it comes down from the Father of lights [the Creator and Sustainer of the heavens], in whom there is no variation [no rising or setting] or shadow cast by His turning [for He is perfect and never changes].

_____

_____

_____

_____

_____

Psalm 145:8-9 (AMP) [8]The Lord is gracious and full of compassion, slow to anger, and abounding in loving kindness. [9]The Lord is good to all, And His tender mercies are over all His works [the entirety of things created].

_____

_____

_____

_____

_____

_____

Psalm 103:8 (AMP) [8]The Lord is merciful and gracious, Slow to anger and abounding in compassion and loving-kindness.

_____

_____

_____

_____

_____

_____

Psalm 84:11 (TPT) [11]For the Lord God is brighter than the brilliance of a sunrise! Wrapping Himself around me like a shield, He is so generous with His gifts of grace and glory. Those who walk along His paths with integrity will never lack one thing they need, for He provides it all!

Psalm 23:6 (KJV) [6]Surely goodness and mercy shall follow me all the days of my life: and I will dwell in the house of the Lord forever.

I don't know about you, but I could go on and on about the goodness of God. He wants His goodness to engulf you. To consume you. Plus, when you focus on the goodness of God, He takes away the fear of evil. When we see His goodness, we can't help but lose sight of the darkness around us. Yes, evil is real, clear, and present. But so is Elohim (God). His goodness engulfs, overcomes, and overshadows evil. His goodness gives you victory over evil. Focus on His goodness! "Get swept up in the goodness of God, and the anointing will flow!"[xlv] The anointing is what penetrates evil and engulfs us in the goodness of God.

Day Six: Failure

The lies we sometimes believe:

I have to be perfect; otherwise, people will not believe in God. I have to keep working even though it's the Sabbath, and I need rest. I can't let others down. I'm not good enough for ministry. Bottom line, I'm not good enough, I'm not qualified, and I have to keep pushing. I have to keep striving.

The truth that sets us free:

Jeremiah 8:4 (AMP)

4"Moreover [Jeremiah], you shall say to them, 'Thus says the Lord, "Do men fall and not rise up again? Does one turn away [from God] and not repent and return [to Him]?

Replacing the lie with the truth:

In the face of failure, many think about taking their lives, as was the case of God's people in this verse. Still, Adonai reassured them He was returning, and He was their avenger. When facing failure, we must not give up because our redeemer lives. He makes us strong. He helps us get back up and try again and again and again.

Time to Decree, Declare, Confess, and Agree:

I decree, declare, confess, and agree with the Word of Elohim. He is my strong tower. He is my compass. When I fail, I will rise again and be the mighty warrior He has called me to be. I am victorious, and everything I do prospers. I am mighty because of Him! He empowers me! He lifts me, dusts me off, and straightens me.

Day Six: The Mark Of Success

There are a lot of theories out there about what success looks like. Is it a bank account that's overflowing with money? Is it a lot of friends? Is it kids who live righteously? Is it a body free from illness? Is it the absence of a lack? Is it a strong influence?

I'm going to say that success is all of the above. When we understand that Adonai says we have everything we need, we lack nothing! Nothing! My friends, He gives us everything we need and sometimes everything we want. There is absolutely no lack in those who know where their real source comes from. The rivers and streams of flowing crystal clear water (wealth) come only from Him, Yâhh (God). He is the real and only source.

In contrast, a person who has a full bank account but their financial transactions are questionable, they are not successful. They, my friends, are in denial. They have no integrity in their finances. Therefore, even if their bank accounts are overflowing, they are in financial lack.

Furthermore, a person can have a lot of friends, but if on their worse days, they don't turn to someone, they hide in shame; they lack personal integrity and transparency. I'm not saying tell everyone your business. I'm saying we need to be vulnerable and authentic. When a person can fully take off their social mask, be susceptible to another person, and be authentic, they are in social abundance. They are a strong influence.

More so, when we identify our success with the success of our children, we're putting the pressure on them. There's a lot of information about emotional incest[xlvi] now than before. In short, it is when the child becomes the parent's best friend or when the child has taken a back seat to the adult. It is essential to practice healthy boundaries with everyone, especially with our children. Parents' success does not equate a child's success and vice versa.

In summary, when our identity is based on how our children turn out or how they are living, we lack true identity. **We need to rest on our oneness with Jesus Christ.** We need to identify with who we genuinely are **IN** Jesus Christ. Who does He say you are? When you have figure out who He says you are, you have found the mark of success.

For day 6, let's look up these verses and write down what does Adonai says about success? If you need additional space, just use a blank paper.

Joshua 1:8, Proverbs 16:3, Matthew 16:26, Psalm 1:1-3, Psalm 37:4

_____

_____

_____

_____

_____

_____

_____

_____

_____

_____

_____

_____

_____

_____

_____

_____

_____

Day Seven: Failing Faith

The lies we sometimes believe:

My faith has halted, it is stagnant, and is failing. What if what I believe is not true? What if Jesus Christ was never a man? I question my faith, and or I have little to no faith.

The truth that sets us free:

Revelation 3:20 (TPT)

[20]Behold, I'm standing at the door, knocking. If your heart is open to hear my voice and you open the door within, I will come into you and feast with you, and you will feast with me.

Replacing the lie with the truth:

Jesus the Christ has unfortunately been blocked from entering many of His churches. He is not welcome in the sanctuaries that long ago were bathed in His love.

To add, many ministers struggle with their faith and even experience bouts of depression. So, they keep Christ, outside of their hearts and outside of their churches. They often struggle in silence due to the fear of others finding out. As Dr. Gary Lovejoy states, "The pastor is expected to minister to others, but who is there to minister to the pastor?"[xlvii] In fact, "Many pastors (and their congregations) believe that it's possible they can fall victim to almost any affliction, except depression."[xlviii] "It's an unwritten rule that people don't want their pastors spiritually victimized or weakened," according to Dr. Gary.

Even further, "To them, it's not only incomprehensible that they're depressed, it's horrifying and humiliating, especially if they have always believed that it's a sign of spiritual weakness."[xlix] So they go through the rituals of Sunday services but have no real intimacy with Jesus Christ.

To add, I can testify because I struggled with my faith. I wanted to keep Jesus Christ at the door and would not let Him in my pain. When I was diagnosed with CRPS,[l] I couldn't understand why it happened to me. It's like my "personal generator"[li] was broken, and God was not willing to fix it.

Before the accident, I was on fire for Jesus Christ. I worshiped, praised, saturated myself in scripture, attended and held Bible studies, and practiced soaking. Soaking is a form of meditating on the presence of the one true God. His presence was honey to my lips. I was immersed in Him. Fully intoxicated with His glory.

After the accident, my heart was closed to Jesus Christ. I practiced the spiritual disciplines and went through the rituals of faith. But my heart was closed. Some call it the dark nights of the soul. "A collapse of a perceived meaning in life."[lii] There were heavy-depressing days full of pain and sorrow. I had to make a choice, agree with what the enemy of my soul was doing to me, or agree with God's word that says He works ALL things for the good of those who love Him.

> # Romans 8:28 (NKJV)
>
> [8]And we know that all things work together for good to those who love God, to those who are called according to His purpose.

In spite of my feelings, physically or emotionally, I confessed my failing faith out loud. I allowed Him to enter into my heart again. My heart was crushed, and it is in the crushing that we experience spiritual promotion. Spiritual promotion only happens when we are genuinely broken. We have to get to a place of brokenness so He can use us. We have to allow the crushing, so we can mature. We become mature in who we are in Him. So, I've learned to enjoy every season of my life. I've learned to embrace the crushing. "How do we know we are making progress? When we wake up and walk around every day knowing deep inside that, we are fully loved and accepted."[liii]

Granted, it is sad when a non-believer doubts, but it is crushing to see a man or woman of God struggle with his or her faith in silence. Struggling in silence is the point I'm trying to make. After all, we are the ones leading the Sheep, Abba's children. We need to confess our failing faith to Him and allow Him to move us out of it.

Still, Christ is faithful to His word and His character. He tells us He is standing at the door. All we have to do (because everyone struggles with their faith at some point), is to allow Him back in. Allow Him into our hearts, homes, churches, in our pain, our brokenness, in our faith. Allow Him to have His way. He is the truth!

He is the Light! He is the King of Kings and Lord of Lords! Jesus Christ is the one true Messiah.

Time to Decree, Declare, Confess, and Agree:

I decree, declare, confess, and agree with Jesus Christ Word when He asks me to let Him in. Jesus Christ, I open my heart to hearing your Word. I open my heart to receive all that you have for me. Fill me, Jesus Christ, with the real revelation of who you are. Flood me with the gift of faith. Fill every space in me that doubts faith. Not faith in faith but faith in you.

I decree, declare, confess, and agree that the Holy Scriptures are breathed by the Ruach HaKodesh through man but breathed through the Spirit.

I decree, declare, confess, and agree that the Holy Trinity is real; The Father, The Son, and The Holy Spirit. You, blessed Trinity, are three in one. I decree, declare, confess, and agree that Adonai is the Lord of Lords and King of Kings.

I decree, declare, confess, and agree that Jesus Christ was born of a virgin. He died for our sins. He rose again in three days and is seated at the right hand of Elohim. I decree, declare, confess, and agree that The Holy Spirit is a person, my friend, counselor, guide, and my comforter. He teaches and moves me.

By faith, I decree, declare, confess, and agree that I am being matured spiritually daily. I will reach perfection when I die. Until then, by faith, I accept I am moving from glory to glory. From victory to victory. By faith, my faith increases daily. In the name of Yeshua HaMashiach, I pray, Amen!

Day Seven: Stable & Grounded Faith

Now, write down what you hear the Lord speaking to you about your faith. He could use; words, signs, visions like a movie scene, a memory from your childhood, and or a snapshot of your future. What is the Lord speaking to you at this moment? Have an honest conversation with Abba about how to have a stable and grounded faith. What does He say it looks like for you?

_____

_____

_____

_____

_____

_____

_____

_____

_____

_____

_____

_____

_____

Let's dig a little deeper. Let's study four people in the Bible who struggled with their faith. Look up these characters. Identify yourself with them. What can you learn from them? Where did their faith fail? How did they overcome their failing faith?

#1. John the Baptist was devoted to his calling and his assignment. He boldly called the Pharisees and Sadducees "brood of vipers[liv]." He did not question his faith. That is until he was in jail. Until he realized his circumstances did not match his expectations. His faith failed him. So much so that he questioned the authority and identity of Jesus Christ. Read the scripture below and ask yourself.... are you questioning Jesus Christ because your circumstances don't match your expectations?

Matthew 11:2-6 (TPT) [2]Now, while John the Baptizer was in prison, he heard about what Christ was doing among the people, so he sent his disciples to ask Him this question: [3]"Are you really the one prophesied would come, or should we still wait for another?" [4]Jesus answered them, "Give John this report: [5]'The blind see again, the crippled walk, lepers are cured, the deaf hear, the dead are raised back to life, and the poor and broken now hear of the hope of salvation!' [6]And tell John that the blessing of heaven comes upon those who never lose their faith in me. - no matter what happens!"

_____

_____

_____

_____

#2. Abraham was chosen by God to be our faith, father. He knew he was called, elected, anointed, cherished, loved, favored, and clearly heard the voice of God. With all of this honey (spiritual blessings) on his life, his faith failed him. He laughed in God's face because he thought that what God was proposing was impossible. As you read the following scripture, ask yourself.... have you ever laughed at what God says He's going to do in you and through you? Have you laughed at God's proposal in your life?

Genesis 17:17 (NKJV) [17]Then Abraham fell on his face and laughed, and said in his heart, "Shall a child be born to a man who is one hundred years old? And shall Sarah, who is ninety years old, bear a child?"

_____

_____

_____

_____

Press a little deeper into this topic. Ask yourself, what has God proposed to you that seems impossible for it to be achieved? What appears too big for God to accomplish? If your faith has failed you, now is the time to ask God to renew your faith. Also, take some time now to repent from agreeing with the enemy who said your faith was failing. Ask The Holy Spirit to walk you through repentance. Ask Him to give you a stable and grounded faith. If you need additional paper just use a blank sheet.

_____

_____

_____

_____

_____

#3. Elijah had a fire breathing faith! He was a Prophet of God. He heard God's voice clearly. His walk matched his talk. His warnings convicted people of returning to the one true God and repent from worshiping false gods. He was on fire for God. That is until the Prophets are being killed[iv] by Jezebel. That's when his faith failed him, and he ran into a cave: see 1 Kings 19:1-7. The man was full of fear! He cowered at the voice, the command, the decree of evil, and wicked spirit. We know in scripture that Elijah returns upon the mandate of the Lord: see 1 Kings 19:15, but his faith had failed him. Ask yourself, what have you, coward, too? What evil spirit has made you run from your fire, breathing faith?

_____

_____

_____

_____

_____

Now ask yourself, what bold step can you take to have a stable and grounded faith? What do you need to face?

_____

_____

_____

_____

#4. The Apostle Peter was the leader of the twelve disciples, the pillar of the faith, and he walked on water. His birth name was Simon, but Jesus Christ renamed him as "Cephas,"[lvi] which translates to Peter, the rock. Peter walked with Jesus Christ. He was one of His closest disciples, the inner circle. Peter knew Jesus Christ intimately. He was his friend, ate with Him, fellowshipped with Him, and stepped out of the boat to be with Him on the water. He witnessed the power and authority of Jesus Christ. One could say his faith was unfailing. That is until Jesus Christ is arrested and taken to be judged by man. The Lord, Jesus Christ, had previously told Peter that he would deny Him, but Peter swore that would never happen. He swore allegiance to Christ until His death. His faith was supposedly solid.

Unfortunately, during that godawful night, when Jesus Christ is arrested, Peter denies Christ. Peter's faith failed him. Peter experience what most of us experience in quiet. His faith failed him. A dark shadow, a failing faith, had engulfed Peter. Fortunately, we know that Peter's faith returns. He becomes the rock the Lord Prophesied he would be. When Christ returned, He redeemed Peter by giving him a mandate, "feed my sheep."[lvii]

Time to get in the Word. Read Luke 22:54-62 and answer these questions:

#1. Why did Peter deny Christ?

_____

_____

_____

_____

#2. Why do you think his faith failed him?

_____

_____

_____

_____

#3. How did Peter bounce back with a stable, grounded, and confident faith?

_____

_____

_____

_____

We've learned that those with what seems to be the most unfailing faith failed at least once. But we've also learned that they bounced back up. If your faith has failed you, confess it to Jesus Christ and allow Him to redeem your faith. No one has gone too far that God can not bring him back. Our faith father laughed at God, and he was still blessed. You and I are no exception; we are redeemed every day.

For this reason, the next time guilt, shame, and or condemnation try to tell you your faith is failing, remind yourself that because of Jesus Christ, you are redeemed. Agree with God that you have a grounded, stable, and confident faith. Your feet are firmly planted on His Word. So, rest knowing He has your faith under control.

Day Eight: No Time For Family

The lies we sometimes believe:

The only family I have is my spiritual family. My immediate family can take a back seat. I don't have time for family because ministry is more important.

The truth that sets us free:

Colossians 3:18-21 (TPT)

[18]Let every wife be supportive and tenderly devoted to her husband, for this is a beautiful illustration of our devotion to Christ. [19]Let every husband be filled with cherishing love for his wife and never be insensitive toward her. [20]Let the children respect and pay attention to their parents in everything for this pleases our Lord Jesus. [21]And fathers don't have unrealistic expectations for your children, or else they may become discouraged.

Replacing the lie with the truth:

When Yâhh created the sacred institute of the family, He knew that a strong bond was going to be needed in the end times. It is the love of a family that holds people together when the days get dark. It is the love of a family that points to the one true God. It is the love of the family that exemplifies the heart of God.

To illustrate, husbands, when you show love to your wife, you are loving Christ. Wives when you respect your husband, you are respecting Christ, Himself.

Similarly, when dishonor and disrespect are present, it is because the spouse is dishonoring Christ. Let me take a moment to speak to the wives only. Wives we are called to show respect to our husband regardless of what they do or don't do. We are not their judge! We are to treat our husbands as if they are Christ in the flesh because they are! Would you talk to Christ the way you speak to your husband?

Moreover, He assigned every member a specific role. When we stay in that role, we complete our assignment. Thereby reaching particular people. The ones we are predestined to reach. If we secure the immediate family first and foremost, we are staying in God's will. We are obedient.

In contrast, when we place the immediate family on the back burner, we are out of God's will. Most, if not all, atheists come from what appear to be healthy Ministry families. They are former preachers kids who never fully recovered from the abandonment, neglect, or painful ministry experience. That is why the family is the first ministry! The family is the engine that keeps the fire burning. The reason why God sent His Son. To showcase mercy, love, grace, and forgiveness. He cares for the family. Do you not realize the Trinity is a family? There is nothing more important than securing the hearts of the family. Also, it is necessary to note that your spiritual family is secondary to your immediate family.

Time to Decree, Declare, Confess, and Agree:

I decree, declare, confess, and agree with Adonai's Word when He placed the family in order. I decree, declare, confess, and agree that family is very essential to Adonai. My immediate family is my first ministry. How I treat my immediate family dictates how much I submit to the one true God. He sees my heart and knows my actions. I decree, declare, confess, and agree that my heart is pure before the Lord and before my family. I decree I give my children the attention they need. I instruct them in the ways of Elohim. I decree, declare, confess, and agree that my spouse is my priority. Ministering to his/her heart is my first battleground. I decree I will not give up on my spouse. He/She will always be covered in prayers. My children will be covered in prayers. I decree my schedule works around the needs of my immediate family.

Abba, thank you for convicting my heart to meet the needs of my immediate family first. Only you move my heart towards them. I praise you because you teach me to love, nurture, care, and provide for my immediate family. You set the order in our home. I praise you because you are an example of a family in order. Have your way Adonai, have your way. In the precious name of Jesus Christ, I pray, Amen!

Day Eight: Family Is A Gift

We are commanded to love others just as Christ loved the church. Our immediate family is the first church we have to minister to. They are our foundational church. We are to love them, embrace them, empower them, and equip them in the way that Abba calls them. Sometimes it doesn't look like the way we want them to go, but Abba has great plans for them. My friends, if we can't minister to our closest loved ones, what makes us think we can minister to others?

Furthermore, when we place our immediate family as a back seat to ministry, we're telling them that other people are more critical. They will inevitably grow in resentment. Again, most atheists are prodigal children of ministers who forgot to put them first place.

We want to be good ambassadors for our family. We want to set good examples for them and make time with them. If we are too busy, we can't spend time with our loved ones, then we're doing ministry wrong! Our immediate family needs us to love them more than our so-called ministry.

Our extended family can also be blessed by our obedience to love them. However, they come in second place to our immediate family. Our extended family is just that an extension of our family. Our spiritual family, as described in the Bible, is our most close-knit family and sometimes can take away from our mission from our biological family. But let us remember, they are saved. We must focus on our immediate family, then our extended family, and then our spiritual family.

Unfortunately, sometimes we have it backward. We spend way too much time with our Sisters and Brothers that we forget to nurture our children, aunts, and uncles. Let us remember we are called to love everyone. Let us put the right relationships in the proper order. Family is a gift that must be treasured and loved. After all, we are ministers of love.

Let us look at some scriptures on the family. As you read the scriptures, ask The Holy Spirit to point out some family members that need to be realigned in your relationship charts. It's time to get the immediate family back in order. It's time to re-prioritize.

Read 1 Timothy 5:8, Ephesians 6:4, Psalm 127:3, and Psalm 128:3.

What do these scriptures say to you about the family and the order of the family?

_____

_____

_____

_____

_____

_____

_____

Let's Talk About Abortion

Friends, I'd like to take this time and talk about abortion. Don't worry, I am not going to condemn you. I want to take this time and share with you that, as an unbeliever, I had three abortions. Two from my first husband. Remember the one who threw me over the rail when I was pregnant with my second daughter. And one from a man who at the time, I thought I truly loved but was afraid of my first husband.

You see, my first husband was in jail when I was in, what I thought was, a serious, committed relationship. When I found out I was pregnant, I had an abortion. I was so afraid of my first husband! Terrified of what would happen to me if he was to find out I was with another man. I was sure he would kill me!

When I became a believer, I carried that guilt, shame, and condemnation of murdering my three children. Sometimes I would justify the abortion to myself by saying it was fear that drove me. Sometimes I would cry endlessly because no one knew. This is the first time I am publicly exposing it outside of Celebrate Recovery. In Celebrate Recovery, my full unabridged testimony is shared.

Indeed, by the grace of God, through CR, healing and deliverance, I was able to release that ungodly guilt. I know my children are in heaven, and one day we will be reunited. I know they are dancing with Jesus Christ and that the pain they suffered at my hand because of the abortion, the Lord wiped it off their minds. Someday we will be reunited for eternity in heaven.

Dear beloved ones, if you have had an abortion, ask the Lord to walk you through repentance. Then ask Him to walk you through forgiving yourself. Then ask Him to walk you through naming your child or children. Then release your guilt to the Lord. Forgive yourself for the abortion. Forgive anyone that accompanied you to get the abortion. Forgive yourself for not knowing what you were doing. If you knew, forgive yourself anyway. Don't let the enemy bind you anymore!

Let's take some time to heal.

First, ask The Holy Spirit to help you and guide you through this inner healing process. Write a confession to Him. Tell Him what you did and why you felt you had to do it. Release the feelings you have been hiding because of the abortion. It is okay to grieve. Permit yourself to grieve. It is okay to cry! Release the tears you have hidden. Now confess.

_____

_____

_____

_____

_____

_____

_____

Second, write down your child's or children's names. Yes, you can name your child with The Holy Spirit's guidance! Let Him help you through this process. Write down your child's or children's names?

_____

_____

_____

_____

_____

Third, ask Jesus Christ to show you your child or children. Remember, they are in heaven. From conception, God had already called them; see Psalm 139:13, Genesis 1:27, and Jeremiah 1:5. So you do not have to worry IF they are in heaven because they are. One day you will be reunited with them. So ask Jesus Christ to show you your child or children. What do you see they are doing?

_____

_____

_____

_____

_____

_____

Fourth, ask Jesus Christ to fill you with hope. Hope that someday you will be reunited. One day your child or children will hug you and tell you that you have been forgiven. There's no guilt, no shame, and no condemnation to those who are in Christ, Jesus. So don't agree with the enemy of your soul anymore! Forgive yourself. Allow Jesus Christ to fill you with hope. Write down what Jesus Christ is telling you at this moment.

_____

_____

_____

_____

_____

_____

_____

_____

_____

_____

_____

_____

My sweet friend, you have now been set free from this lie that has bound you! Rejoice! You are Free!

Day Nine: Fear

The lies we sometimes believe:

I am afraid of this pandemic. I am afraid of what people will think or say. I'm so scared to start something new or stop something old. I have been hurt before, so I am afraid of others. Some people, animals, or things give me fear. What will people think if they knew the truth about my family, my business, or my ministry? I'm afraid! Fear has gripped me. It has crippled me. Fear is real, and I can not deny it.

The truth that sets us free:

Isaiah 14:3 (KJV)
³And it shall come to pass in the day that the Lord shall give thee rest from thy sorrow, and from thy fear, and from the hard bondage wherein thou was made to serve,

Replacing the lie with the truth:

God knows the tight grip fear has on His children. Fear is an entity. Still, His Word says He will give us rest. We can be confident He will deliver us. He has seen our bondage, but He has also seen and created our victory.

So, next time fear squeezes tight, remind **it** that Jesus Christ' Blood has killed its power. Call its bluff and take it to Adonai. Repent from agreeing with fear. Renounce its power. Curse and break it. Confess to Adonai. Receive Adonai's forgiveness. Release Adonai's goodness over it. Praise and worship Adonai because He is your Deliverer. He slew the beast once and for all! Now, all we have to do is disagree with it and agree with Adonai.

Time to Decree, Declare, Confess, and Agree:

I decree, declare, confess, and agree with the Word of Adonai that says, You did not give me a spirit of fear but of power, love, and a sound mind.[lviii] I decree Abba, you are the spirit that dwells within me. I decree your Spirit empowers me to complete all that you have assigned for me. I decree I do not fear man's opinion. I decree I finish all that you have birthed within me. I decree I do not fear being hurt by others. I rest on your unfailing eternal love. I decree unholy fear is now evicted from me. Holy fear warns me to move from a dangerous person, place, or thing. Unholy fear stops me from growing, so I renounce it now, in Jesus Christ's name. Unholy fear has no seat in me. In the name of Jesus Christ.

I decree, declare, confess, and agree I walk with transparency and no translucency. My family, ministry, and business are consecrated to serve you, Adonai. Everything is in your hands, you control it all. You hide me from the schemes of the enemy. You reveal the works of the flesh. You protect me; therefore, I shall not fear. I walk in victory in the name of Jesus Christ.

I decree, declare, confess, and agree, fear has now lost its grip on me. By the Blood of the Lamb, I am now set free! I walk in pure Holy Freedom! In the name of Yeshua HaMashiach, I pray all these things, Amen!

Day Nine: Fearless Assertion

During the printing stage of this book, there was a worldwide pandemic. Unprecedented events began to unfold. Countries closed their borders. Church's closed their sanctuaries. Schools and some government offices were closed. People were forced isolated. People panicked shopped and emptied the store shelves. There was a mass spread of hoarding. People were fighting over the basics like toilet paper. Almost everyone was crippled with Fear!

Yes, fear can be crippling. It is a spirit that has dominated even the best of us. It has and continues to hold many in captivity. Sadly, many stay in those spiritual chains bound. They don't know how to face it. They never learn to see the spirit of fear. Some have died because they do not realize they can be set free.

In fact, that is why I am here today to confess that I have fought this spirit. Like many, I have faced it's ugly head and have battled with it. It is a controlling, manipulative, and domineering spirit. It is only here to kill, steal, and destroy you and yours. But fear not! The King of Kings and Lord of Lords is for us. He equips us.

For example, Adonai has equipped us with many great tools to overcome this ugly spirit. He is not going to leave us weaponless in a world that is under the power and authority of the enemy of humankind. He left us tools. Tools that are at our disposal. All we have to do is ask for His tools.

Now, let's study some verses that talk about the tools we have to face this ugly spirit of fear. It's not all of our arsenals, but it's the best weaponry we have.

As you read the scriptures, ask yourself these questions; How can you apply them to your fears? Then, write the truth as it applies to you. Make decrees, declarations, confessions, and agreements with the Word.

2 Corinthians 10:4, Ephesians 6:10-18, Isiah 59:16-19

_____

_____

_____

_____

_____

_____

_____

_____

_____

_____

_____

Day Ten: Financial Loss

The lies we sometimes believe:

My mom was poor, my daddy was poor, and my siblings are poor; therefore, I will always be poor. Poverty is in our veins, so I will never make enough money. Why even try if I'm still broke! It is a blessing and a testament of humbleness to be in poverty. I work and work and work and can never get ahead.

The truth that sets us free:

Deuteronomy 8:18 (NIV)

[18]But remember the Lord your God, for it is He who gives you the ability to produce wealth, and so confirms His covenant, which He swore to your ancestors, as it is today.

Replacing the lie with the truth:

No matter what we think or feel about our financial situation, Abba made a covenant with our ancestors to secure our financial freedom. When we trust Him, of course, He will provide the wealth of heaven and teach us to steward it. When we place our finances at His feet, He's a better manager than we could ever be.

Time to Decree, Declare, Confess, and Agree:

Abba, I decree, declare, confess, and agree, I do not fear financial loss or financial bondage. Your Word confirms a covenant YOU made with my ancestors. You took it upon yourself to see that me and mine will be financially blessed. I decree, declare, confess, and agree that YOU are my banker. I decree, declare, confess, and agree that I rest, knowing you are a better financial manager than I could ever be.

Abba, thank you for being my dependable financial provider. Thank you for paying my bills. Thank you for your provision. Thank you for taking care of the monetary problems that I can't even see. Thank you, because I can rest knowing you have my back. Thank you for securing an overflow for me and mine. You have acquired a legacy for me and mine. Wealth is the inheritance of your children.

Abba, I agree with YOUR word in Deuteronomy 8:18, you give me the ability to produce wealth, YOU confirm the covenant! You take responsibility for my finances. Thank you, Abba! Thank you!

Only you are worthy, Holy, and mighty! I bless you, Abba, in Jesus Christ's name, I pray, Amen!

Day Ten: Kingdom Prosperity Is His Provision

When we understand that prosperity is not blasphemy, and we stop cursing our finances, we can receive the fullness of His wealth. It's all His! All the money in the world belongs to Abba. No matter how much we want to kid ourselves, we can't work into prosperity. It comes from above! It comes from living under the reality that He owns it all.

> ## Colossians 1:16 (NIV)
>
> [16]For in Him all things were created: things in heaven and on earth, visible and invisible, whether thrones or powers or rules or authorities; all things have been created through Him and for Him.

Since Elohim created the heavens and the earth, then He owns it all. Everything, ALL, the fullness of the land is His, the entire universe belongs to Him, the totality of the space we occupy belongs to Him.

Therefore, since He created everything and everything belongs to Him, then the money, of course, belongs to Him. And yes, there is a family out there that claim they own it all. However, scripture is unambiguous, He dominates it ALL! So trust Him with your finances. Trust His leading!

Stop being afraid of the word prosperity. For your information, this is not prosperity theology. This is provision teaching. This is the full provision from Abba that leads to Kingdom wealth. This is teaching you to clear your mind of the lies that hold you captive to financial bondage. You were created to prosper. Let The Holy Spirit guide you on how to thrive. Study these verses and apply them to your prosperity. What do these scriptures tell you about God's provision and His wealth?

Deuteronomy 28:11-12, Proverbs 10:22, 2 Corinthians 9:8, Philippians 4:19, John 10:10

_____

_____

_____

_____

_____

_____

_____

_____

_____

Friends, when we understand that God wants us to prosper for His namesake, we can let go and allow Him to work. Here are some Bible characters that testify to God's provision, His abundance, and some points to ponder on.

1. Adam and Eve were instructed to increase (abundance). They were supposed to subdue the earth. We are their children and carry that same responsibility. We are to expand, grow in abundance, and conquer the planet. See Genesis 1:28-30

2. Abram and Sarai were called out of their comfort zone and into a land they did not know, the area of the Canaan's. Through their obedience, not only were they renamed, but they became the parents to many nations. The Lord renamed them, Abraham and Sarah. At 99 years old, He, the Lord, added "Hamon" meaning multitude, crowd,[lix] to Abraham. They had the responsibility to carry out abundance to the nations through their faith. The Lord declared Abraham was a blessing. We are their heirs. We have received those blessings.

3. Apostle Paul formerly known as Saul of Tarsus, was a tentmaker: see Acts 18:1-4. In today's terminology, he would be considered an entrepreneur. Paul knew that he had the blessings of God. Not once in scripture do we read that Paul ever worried about finances. He knew God was going to provide because the ultimate goal of wealth is to advance the Kingdom. God's Kingdom, not our kingdom. So if we are using our finances to bring honor and glory to God, guess what, they will be blessed.

4. The Lord provides wealth because He is our Father. What Father would not provide for their children? See Matthew 7:11.

5. The Lord provides wealth so we can be of influence. People can trust someone who has had experience, competence, is of good character, and testimony of walking in wisdom.

6. The Lord provides wealth to transform generations. Many call this revival. Yet, we can't have revivals if everyone is broke. We are called to be shifters, change agents, revival breakers, and, when needed, bring reformation.

As you can see, there's no reason to think anything less than Kingdom Prosperity and Kingdom Provision. It all belongs to Him, and He wants to release it to you.

Again this is not a prosperity Theology. This is provision teaching. It is about learning to stand under the blessings of Yâhh.

Proverbs 28:6 (AMP)
⁶Better is the poor who walks in
his integrity. Than he who is
crooked and
two-faced though he is rich.

Day Eleven: Foolishness

The lies we sometimes believe:

I am stupid! Nothing I do will ever change my circumstances. I'm just not good enough.

The truth that sets us free:

Philippians 1:9-11 (AMP)

[9]And this I pray, that your love may abound more and more [displaying itself in greater depth] in real knowledge and in practical insight, [10]so that you may learn to recognize and treasure what is excellent [identifying the best, and distinguishing more differences], and that you may be pure and blameless until the day of Christ [actually living lives that lead others away from sin]; [11]filled with the fruit of righteousness which comes through Jesus Christ, to the glory and praise of God [so that His glory may be both revealed and recognized].

Replacing the lie with the truth:

The Apostle Paul prayed for God's children to be full of real knowledge and real wisdom. When you focus on the fact, which is you have "real" wisdom, you immediately cancel the lie of foolishness.

Time to Decree, Declare, Confess, and Agree:

I decree, declare, confess, and agree that I have real knowledge and real insight from heaven. I decree, declare, confess, and agree that I recognize and treasure the excellence within me and around me. I decree, declare, confess, and agree that I am made pure and blameless.

I decree, declare, confess, and agree that I am filled with the fruit of righteousness. I decree, declare, confess, and agree that He gets ALL the glory and all the praise. He is the King of Kings, the Lord of Lords, the Alpha, and the Omega. I decree He gives me the right mind of Jesus Christ. There is nothing in my mind that is missing, and there is nothing broken. I cancel the lie of foolishness in the name of Jesus Christ. I rest knowing, He redeems my mind. In Jesus Christ's mighty name, I pray, Amen!

Day Eleven: Godly Wisdom

It is essential to state that there are levels of cognitive abilities. Psychologists, Doctors, Therapists, Coaches, and even Mentors (Christian and non-Christian) have made a living out of telling people what they can and cannot do. We do understand that a person's chronological age may not necessarily match their cognitive age.

For example, a fact is a chronological 15 years old might have a 5-year old's cognitive ability. Factually, some people suffer from intellectual impairment. A fact is, an adult may function with the limited capacity of a child. Those are facts. We do not deny the "facts," man's facts, to be precise.

Conversely, we look at scripture. What does God say about my child's cognitive ability? Where in scripture does it say that my child is limited in his abilities? More on this topic will be shared in the coming days.

Despite the professional diagnosis, our diagnosis, and or the world's diagnosis, we have to look at scripture. When we feel foolish in our ways or that our loved ones are being foolish, or they are cognitively foolish, we must remember, scripture has the final word. The final diagnosis. We use scripture to combat those foolish thoughts and replace them with Abba's thoughts. We ask Him for His wisdom. We ask Him for His mind. We ask Him for His thoughts.

Time to put some meat in our words. Let's study these scriptures. Write down foolishness you have believed. Then write down the truth that God says according to the scripture. Then write down a decree, declaration, confession, and agreement with the scripture.

James 1:5 (HCSB) ⁵Now, if any of you lacks wisdom, he should ask God, who gives to all generously and without criticizing, and it will be given to him.

_____

_____

_____

_____

_____

Proverbs 16:16 (TPT) ¹⁶Everyone wants gold, but wisdom's worth is far greater. Silver is sought after, but a heart of understanding yields a greater return.

_____

_____

_____

_____

_____

Proverbs 8:11 (NIV) [11]for wisdom is more precious than rubies, and nothing you desire can compare with her.

_____

_____

_____

_____

_____

_____

Proverbs 4:6-7 (TPT) [6]Stick with wisdom, and she will stick to you, protecting you throughout your days. She will rescue all those who passionately listen to her voice. [7] Wisdom is the most valuable commodity - so buy it! Revelation knowledge is what you need – so invest in it!

_____

_____

_____

_____

_____

_____

Day Twelve: Forgetting & Mental Health

The lies we sometimes believe:

I was diagnosed with a permanent mental illness; mood disorder, eating disorder, borderline personality disorder, cognitive and developmental disorder, anxiety disorder, Psychotic disorder, Substance abuse disorder, physical disorder, dependent personality disorder, paranoid personality disorder, obsessive-compulsive personality disorder, histrionic personality disorder, schizotypal personality disorder, schizoid personality disorder, narcissistic personality disorder, bipolar disorder, and or borderline personality disorder. There is no cure for this cognitive condition.

The truth that sets us free:

1 Corinthians 2:16 (AMP)
[16]For who has known the mind and purposes of the Lord so as to instruct him? But we have the mind of Christ [to be guided by His thoughts and purposes].

Replacing the lie with the truth:

Upon our salvation, we died and were born again. There was a funeral for our old mind. Our diagnostic mind was crucified, and our right mind of Jesus Christ was embedded. We have the right mental state that is the cognitive state of our Lord Jesus Christ. He takes it upon Himself to redeem our minds. We don't look at mankind for his approval of our mental state. We look at the Word of Adonai and rest on His infallible Word. For this purpose, we must renew our minds **daily** with the Word of God, His infallible Word.

Time to Decree, Declare, Confess, and Agree:

I decree, declare, confess, and agree with Elohim's Word that states I have the mind of Christ. My brain does not conform to the patterns of this world. It is transformed by the constant renewing of His Word. Psalm 107:20 says I am healed and delivered. In Jeremiah 33:6 says there is peace and truth in my mind. In Zephaniah 3:17, He quiets my mind with His song. He gently whispers through Mark 5:34 that my faith has healed me, completely!

I decree, declare, confess, and agree He is the Lord who heals me as His Word says in Exodus 15:26.

I decree, declare, confess, and agree He restores my mind. He heals ALL my wounds. He has declared it, so I agree!

I decree, declare, confess, and agree that my mind is in perfect peace because it is steadfast on Him, and I trust in Him!

I decree, declare, confess, and agree with 2 Timothy 1:7 that states Elohim has not given me a spirit of fear. But He has given me The Holy Spirit, which is a Spirit of power, love, and a sound mind. The Holy Spirit lives inside of me. The Holy Spirit pulls down any spirit that tries to exalts its self against Him.

I decree, declare, confess, and agree that The Holy Spirit delivers my mind from ungodly thoughts, ungodly diagnoses, ungodly communions, confusions, ungodly covenants, faulty foundations, and the carnal mind. Greater is The Holy Spirit that lives in me than he who is in the world. In the name of Yeshua HaMashiach, I pray, Amen!

Day Twelve: Holy Blessed Memory

"The blood of Jesus cleanses us from all sin so that the negative seeds that we or others have planted in us can die."[ix] Hallelujah! Praise Elohim! He burns up any ungodly seed. We remember we are His! We remember we are seated in heavenly places. We recognize that no weapon formed against us shall prosper. We admit that No weapon means no diagnosis, no tests, no injuries, no plots, no ungodly seeds, no ploys, and or no schemes. Nothing formed against us shall prosper. We have The Holy Spirit residing in us and working through us. We have the power of all power.

In other words, when we get a diagnosis, we test it against the Word of Elohim. What does His Word say about it? Does He give you that diagnosis? Does scripture testify to the diagnosis? If it does not, don't receive it, throw it away. Don't let it seep into your spirit. Don't let it into your heart. In Proverbs 4:23, the Lord tells us to guard our hearts.

Since our hearts hold the keys to life and death, we must guard it. We can not allow outside forces to dictate it. Our heart carries the "physical and emotional-intellectual-moral"[lxi] compass and functions.

For example, what we believe in our hearts, we manifest in our bodies. Our heart is a very potent muscle that, if left unchecked, can bring us the destruction the enemy of humankind seeks for us. So, when we receive a diagnosis that does not align with scripture, let us check our heart and command it to align with scripture.

Let us disagree with the enemy of humankind who seeks to only kill, steal, and destroy us and let us agree with the Word of Adonai. Adonai is the Hebrew name for God. It is the plural of Adonai, meaning "Lord, Lord, LORD, Master, or owner."[lxii] He is the Master, He has the final word and the definitive diagnosis.

As a further matter, if Adonai is the King of Kings, Lord of Lords, Master of Masters and Owner of Owners, don't you think He wants nothing but the best for you? He commands the enemy to take his hands off of you when you are living righteously and have the faith that moves mountains.

John 14:30 (AMP)

[30]I will not speak with you much longer, for the ruler of the world (satan) is coming. And he has no claim on Me [no power over Me nor anything that he can use against Me]

In other words, if the enemy of humankind has no claim on you, then he has to take back that diagnosis. If he does have a claim on you, just repent, turn from that wickedness and allow The Holy Spirit to guide you to the truth. Ask The Holy Spirit to guide you through repentance. You are His beloved child, He wants to heal you of ALL your iniquities and diseases, ailments, and diagnosis.[lxiii]

Now it's time to allow yourself to do a spiritual inventory, a heart check. Where are your thoughts? Where are your actions? Does your talk match your walk? Is there any iniquity in you? Have you given or taken any offense? Have you forgiven? Do you feel the need to control; situations, events, and or people? Are you honest with yourself and others? Do you beat yourself up over the poor choices you've made? Do you feel like a failure? Are you hard on yourself or others? Do you have impure thoughts? Can you be selfish at times? Is your love sometimes conditional? Is there resentment in you? Do you feel unholy guilt? Is there any fear in you? Is there sinful pride in you? Have you looked deep in your soul?

As you meditate on the previous questions ask The Holy Spirit to look in your heart. Permit Him to search within you. Permit Him to sift you. Permit Him to sit with you through this process.

Now, write down what you are feeling, sensing, or hearing. Release anything the enemy of your soul is using against you. Release anything that can be a block to your healing. Release those ungodly covenants, actions, motivations, reactions, and suppression. Unhook yourself from the enemy of your soul

It's time to be truthful to Holy Spirit, your brother Jesus Christ, and your Father-Abba. He wants to walk with you through this process. It's time to take off your mask. Reread the previous questions and work thru them. It's crucial to write down your confessions so that you can get them off of your soul. As you write, if you need more space, just use a separate piece of paper.

Remember to ask The Holy Spirit to stay connected with you as you release your confessions.

Day Thirteen: Twisted Future

The lies we sometimes believe:

No need to make plans because the future is hopeless. This world has fallen apart. We're living in the last days, so why bother. The government controls me. No matter what I do, I just can't get ahead.

The truth that sets us free:

Romans 15:13 (HCSB)
[13]Now may the God of hope fill you with all joy and peace as you believe in Him so that you may overflow with hope by the power of The Holy Spirit.

Replacing the lie with the truth:

When we feel hopeless about our future, we can trust Adonai. He says He will overflow us with hope. Hope for a future, a vibrant future. So let's take Him up on His Word because He can not lie.

Time to Decree, Declare, Confess, and Agree:

I decree, declare, confess, and agree with the Word of God when He says I am filled with His hope. He fills me up! He gives me the confidence I need to plan for the future. Though this world is wicked, I am not of this world. I am seated in heavenly places. I agree with Romans 15:13, the power of The Holy Spirit overflows me with hope. I have hope inside of me, and I give hope to others. I am a hope carrier.

Day Thirteen: Perfectly Created Destiny

Everyone has a destiny, a purpose, and a God-given vision. When the Lord created us in the belly of our mother's, He planted something inside of us. When He was weaving our nose, ears, and eyes, He whispered a destiny, a purpose, a vision, and a plan.

Obviously, the enemy of humankind will whisper the opposite. He will whisper that the future is hopeless. He will whisper all kinds of destruction. Even manipulates you into not planning because after all, the world is going to end, right?! He will try to negate every plan you make. Even derailing you from planning. He will keep you occupied with mindless tasks. Like, scrolling away from your life.

Indeed, he is the father of ALL lies. Nothing that comes out of his mouth is ever right. NOTHING! So what is his tactic against you? The enemy of your soul won't straight out lie to you. Remember, during Jesus Christ's temptation (see Matthew 4:3), he said, "If," "if." He tries to question God and the validity of the scriptures. He does not deny who Jesus Christ is, but he's probing Jesus Christ. The enemy of our souls wants to "break the hold the Word of God has on us."[lxiv]

Although satan whispers a wicked future, God has birthed a perfect destiny. Read your Bible every day. I mean literally every day. I know it sounds cliché, but it's true. As you read the Word, you learn to combat his lies and immerse yourself in the truth. The truth that there is hope for the future!

Now it's time to wash our brains from the belief that the future is hopeless. In Daniel 12:2-3, we get a glimpse of everlasting life and that we will shine like the brightness of heaven. Why would God say that if we didn't have a destiny? Ask yourself, as you look up the scripture, read it, and meditate on it; why would I have everlasting life?

_____

_____

_____

_____

_____

Ask yourself, what is the divine intersection of where I am to where God wants me to be? What does my spiritual hallway look like? Am I fighting the process or growing from it?

_____

_____

_____

_____

_____

When we search for God, He leads us to our ideal future. Our perfect future is found in the day to day grind. The planning, the expecting, and the rejoicing. Rejoicing because we get to be partakers of this world. We get to be part of the healing of this world. What can you do to help heal this world? Are you establishing your identity in Jesus Christ? Are you obedient to His Word and His mandate for you?

_____

_____

_____

_____

_____

_____

_____

Clearly, we are living in the last of the last days. Look up Matthew 24:37-39, Luke 17:28-30, Genesis 6:5, 11, 12, and Jude 1:7. What did God say about the end times? Write down a quick summary of what you learned from these scriptures.

_____

_____

_____

_____

_____

_____

Since we are in the end times, the Lord has given us a garment of righteousness. Let's look at some scriptures that talk about the clothing of righteousness. As you read the scriptures, ask yourself how you can impact the end times generations? Are you clutching to your garment of righteousness? Why or why not?

Isaiah 61:10, Revelation 3:18, Genesis 3:21, Galatians 3:27

Day Fourteen: Hell

The lies we sometimes believe:

There is absolutely no hell! Hell is for bad people only. I'm a good person, so I will not go to hell. Hell is propaganda to manipulate the masses.

The truth that sets us free:

Matthew 13:42 (KJV)
[42]And shall cast them into a furnace of fire: there shall be wailing and gnashing of teeth.

Replacing the lie with the truth:

One of the greatest deceptions of the accuser of the brethren (the enemy of humankind), is to have people think there is no hell. But Abba's Word clearly states there is a hell. We can trust Abba's word. If it tells us there's a hell, guess what, there's a hell. And it is not a beautiful, squishy, happy or inviting place to be in. It's a furnace fire with wailing and gnashing of teeth. There's never-ending torment. There's no hope, no future, no light. But fear not for Adonai has blessed us with Salvation. Salvation from hell. His Salvation is an open invitation to all.

Time to Decree, Declare, Confess, and Agree:

I agree with the Word of Adonai that there is a hell. I confess that hell is for the unsaved. I decree, declare, confess, and agree that I am saved by the Blood of the Lamb and the word of my testimony.

In case you are wondering what we need to be **saved from**? Ask yourself:

If you have ever stolen, cheated, lied, lusted, exaggerated, embellished, committed adultery (in the mind as well), watched pornography, fornicated (sex without marriage), hated, held bitterness, disobeyed, treated someone badly, committed corruption, coveted (felt jealousy), were rebellious, felt rejection (or rejected someone), felt condemnation (or condemned someone), had little gods that took your attention away from what really mattered in your life (internet), used drugs, said a white lie, committed a blue/white collar crime, had gluttony, greed, were lazy, had a slumbering spirit, were sloth, had a nasty attitude, had envy, felt prideful, felt a need to get vengeance, murdered (abortion as well), lived in denial about a situation, disrespected your father or your mother, disrespected your neighbor/family, neglected family/friends, did not value the need for rest, over worked, under worked, did not sleep enough to reboot your brain, did not fellowship (invested in someone else life), lied on someone, tried to commit suicide, lived under fear, tried to isolate, felt rage, felt anger, felt apathy, co-depended on others, spoke profanity, manipulated, cheated on your taxes, were combative, and or felt unworthy........... You need to be saved from hell, the eternal damnation!

You need to be forgiven! You need to forgive! You need to be saved from the choices and words you have said over yourself and over other people. You need Jesus Christ to come into your life and help you get back on the right path. The path that leads to eternal life full of peace. You need to be saved from you and the world.

I repeat you need to be saved from you and the world. This is also known as sinful nature. Your sinful nature causes you to make wrong choices. It causes you to have mixed emotions, and your moral compass gets discombobulated. All of these emotions, sins, actions, and reactions currently condemn you to a place that is away from peace, love, and joy. It is ETERNAL DAMNATION! ETERNAL! It is a place that was created for the fallen angels, aka the enemy of humankind and his posse. Abba did not create this place for His creation. We are His creation. That place of eternal damnation is called Sheol.

> Psalm 139:8 (AMP)
> [8]If I ascend to heaven, You are there;
> If I make my bed in Sheol (the nether world, the place of the dead),
> behold, You are there.

Sheol is also known as hell. It is the place where the permanently dead abide. They are tortured continuously. They experience unimaginable pain and suffering. There's fear, isolation, darkness, incomprehensible thirst, burning of the souls over and over. Literally the worst place imaginable. There's no return trip from hell.

In short, the Lords' hand is not in Sheol. Neither is His presence. People get tormented for decades upon decades upon decades without an end in sight. They experience unimaginable thirst. It has been said that people are torn apart over and over and over again. They scream because of the inexplicable fear and pain. It's been shared that the darkness is so thick there is no air passing through it. The dark is so palpable that you can't see another living being. Still, you can hear other people screaming, begging for help. Soul's scream as they are chained and tortured repeatedly. The demons are angry, hostile, and full of hate for creation. They hate us! In Sheol, they have no pity or remorse. Reiterating, it is literally the worst place you can think of!

Abba's presence, heartbeat, love, mercy, grace, and forgiveness is NOT in Sheol. Souls stay in bondage permanently in Sheol. Please hear me, Abba is not in Sheol! Even if for a brief second you don't believe there is a God, consider there is a hell. Picture hell in your mind and imagine if you want your loved ones to be tortured over and over. With no mercy or end in sight. Then cry out to the Father and ask Him to help you believe. He will help you because He wants to help you! He wants to save you!

For more testimonies on hell, you can google Mary K Baxter Ministries.[lxv] She explains her trip with Jesus Christ to hell. Only with Jesus Christ's leading can you go and return from this experience. You can also follow Bill Wiese[lxvi], he also went to hell. You can search for many more true-account testimonies. From a personal perspective, the Lord Jesus Christ took me on several occasions to heaven. But He also took me to hell. I will share more about this, perhaps at another time. Let's not lose focus; it's all about Jesus Christ!

Now, the opposite state for the permanently dead is eternal life. Our physical bodies perish, but with God, as our savior, we experience eternal life. You and your household get to be in a place where love, joy, peace, goodness, and kindness abide. A place flowing with milk and honey. A place where the presence of the Lord is always there. A place of true fullness. A place where you never suffer, never cry, never fear, never feel alone. A place of pure **abounding love**. The opposite of the current life you now have.

Day Fourteen: Radiance Of Heaven

Opposite of Hell is heaven. Heaven is the city of God's home. The dwelling of His presence. There's no need for a sun or a moon because His presence illuminates it. Sickness and diseases do not exist. Heaven is beautiful, with many colors, no man can describe. Animals and humans co-exist without the desire to kill each other. People play with their loved ones without any fears. Children run around full of innocence. Heaven is like nothing we can imagine here on earth. It is peaceful! Now let's look at some more truths about heaven.

First, the Bible gives us the exact measurements of heaven.

Revelation 21:16 (TPT) ¹⁶The city was laid out in a perfect square; it's length, width, and height were equal. So he measured the city with his rod, and it was 12,000 stadia, with equal dimensions for its width, length, and height.

Second, Jesus Christ tells us He's going there to prepare a place for us.

John 14:1-3 (AMP) ¹"Do not let your heart be troubled (afraid, cowardly). Believe [confidently] in God and trust in Him, [have faith, hold on to it, rely on it, keep going and] believe also in Me. ²In my Father's house are many dwelling places. If it were not so, I would have told you, because I am going there to prepare a place for you. ³And if I go and prepare a place for you, I will come back again and I will take you to Myself so that where I am you may be also.

Third, the Bible gives us testimonies of heaven and people taken to heaven.

1 John 5:7 (KJV) [7]For there are three that bear record in heaven, the Father, the Word, and the Holy Ghost: and these three are one.

Genesis 5:24 (NIV) [24]Enoch walked faithfully with God; then he was no more because God took him away.

2 Kings 2:11 (AMP) [11]As they continued along and talked, behold, a chariot of fire with horses of fire [appeared suddenly and] separated the two of them, and Elijah went up to heaven in a whirlwind.

Fourth and final, Serah, daughter of Asher.[lxvii] Who is only mentioned in the English Bible versions three times: see Genesis 46:17, Numbers 26:46, and 1 Chronicles 7:30. But is mentioned in the Hebrew Midrash[lxviii] as having been blessed by Jacob with eternal life. Meaning she will never die. According to the Hebrew Torah, she was lifted in a chariot of fire.

Clearly, heaven is a physical place, Jesus Christ testifies He lives there, and people have been taken to heaven without dying. We can safely say, yes, there is a heaven. So we know Hell is real and heaven is real too.

Now it's time we dig our nails into scriptures. We're going to look at some verses on hell. Take your time to meditate on each scripture because we're going to kill the lie of the enemy that says hell is not a real place. Look up these scriptures. Read them specially out loud, and ask yourself, can you confess and agree that hell exists? Why or why not? Then write a decree, declaration, confession and agreement with the Word.

Revelation 21:8

_____

_____

_____

_____

Matthew 13:50

_____

_____

_____

_____

Matthew 25:41

Revelation 19:20

_____

_____

_____

_____

_____

Matthew 10:28

_____

_____

_____

_____

Matthew 25:46

_____

_____

_____

_____

Day Fifteen: Illness

The lies we sometimes believe:

My illness brings honor and glory to Adonai. If God wanted to heal me, He would have. I will always be barren. I deserve this illness. I'm taking this illness on for someone else. There's no cure for what I have. I was born sick; therefore, I will die sick. God can not heal me. This is an incurable illness.

The truth that sets us free:

Isaiah 53:5 (HCSB)
⁵But He was pierced because of our transgressions, crushed because of our iniquities; punishment for our peace was on Him, and we are healed by His wounds.

Replacing the lie with the truth:

In the Old Testament, it was prophesied that Jesus Christ was going to be crucified. Still, Christ willingly laid His life down so that by His wounded body and the shedding of His Blood, we would be healed. The Word says we are healed. It is not suggesting it, it is declaring it! We are healed, whole, and delivered.

Time to Decree, Declare, Confess, and Agree:

I decree, declare, confess, and agree that by Christ the Messiah's, stripes I am healed! I decree, declare, confess, and agree that I heed to the Word of Adonai. I agree with His Word that speaks life and health to my body. I agree and activate my faith by hearing of His Word. I agree His Word will manifest because Elohim, watches for His Word. I decree I boldly approach His throne of grace and mercy, where I plead the Blood of Jesus Christ for my healing manifestation. I decree, declare, confess, and agree that the Lord is my healer, my defense, and my Father.

<repeat this until it seeps into your heart>

I decree, declare, confess, and agree that Jehovah Rapha is my healer! I decree, declare, confess, and agree that Jehovah Rapha is my healer! I decree, declare, confess, and agree that Jehovah Rapha is my healer! I DECREE, DECLARE, CONFESS, AND AGREE THAT JEHOVAH RAPHA IS MY HEALER!

<repeat this until it seeps into your heart>

I decree, declare, confess, and agree that healing is mine because of the finished work of the cross by Jesus Christ and His Blood. By the Blood of the Lamb, I am healed! By the Blood of the Lamb, I am healed! By the Blood of the Lamb, I am healed! BY THE BLOOD OF THE LAMB, I AM HEALED!

I agree with His Word, He never lies. His Word is pure, authentic, tested, and never returns void. His Word is my life insurance. His Word is my estate. His Word is my diagnosis. His Word is my healing!

Day Fifteen: Wellness & Whole

On September 21, 2019, as I was soaking and meditating on Jesus Christ, He came to my room. He laid His hands on my foot and said I was healed. My body started to convulse and started to fight off His healing. Then Jesus Christ began to wash my foot. His compassion brought me to tears. Then He said to me that I was now healed. He said that the next time the enemy of my soul lies to me about my healing for me to remind him that Jesus Christ has washed my foot.

So, I believe, by faith, that on this day, I received my healing. Though I do not have a medical clearance saying I am healed. And the physical manifestations of the illness are still here, for example, pain, burning from within, and swollen limbs, I stand on Jesus Christ's Word, I am healed! I decree, declare, confess, and agree with Jesus Christ, I AM HEALED!

Furthermore, when we fully immerse ourselves in the Word of God, we can see that healing is ours by the Blood of the Lamb. When Jesus Christ went to the cross, He paid for our healing. He became our doctor, bore our diseases, slew the diagnosis, cursed the ailments, and killed the viruses. He removed the spirit of infirmity. He healed us! It's a done deal!

Albeit, yes, it's a hard concept to understand when the world is telling us we're full of diagnosis. Some diagnosis seems incurable. Some diagnosis are too forceful for our minds to believe we will be healed. We experience unimaginable suffering. But "God uses the trials, tribulations and yes, sufferings, of daily life to break up our soulish hindrances toward His Spirit."[lxix]

So, that's when we press into the spiritual disciplines. We need to cancel out "Doubt, Disbelieve, and Disobedience."[lxx] Reading over scriptures that defy what the world is telling us. Saturating ourselves with healing scriptures. Which is the truth! Soaking our atmosphere with His presence, His glory, His love, His compassion! "In the New Testament, Christ revealed that time for healing was always now."[lxxi]

Furthermore, that's the perfect time to press into the "celebration of discipline."[lxxii] When we engage in the spiritual disciplines, we're not working for our healing. We are training our bodies to submit to the authority of the Word of Jesus Christ. We're training our bodies to submit to The Holy Spirit. We're training our bodies to accept the truth and renounce the lie. We are reprogramming our souls; the mind, will, emotions, and spirit. "Don't allow the enemy to claim what is legally and Scripturally yours."[lxxiii]

"What the Bible will do for you
depends
on how you receive it.
If you receive it
as a word of man,
it will not work it's full working.
However,
if you receive it as
the Word of God,
it will work effectively
in you."
Paraphrasing Derek Prince

Besides, doctors have made claims that viruses are out of their control, and medicine may not be the rescue that they once were. They have made claims such as "we're just creating this monster."[lxxiv] "Medicine is, and always has been, an evolving discipline"[lxxv] and" "Virtually all of our medical therapeutic options are being questioned, evaluated and re-evaluated by researchers across the globe."[lxxvi] Even the FDA has a "black box" of medication. The link to 2018 & 2019's FDA's black box list is in the end-notes.

Therefore, if doctors are admitting they cannot cure all the diseases all the time because of the evolving viruses, who do we trust? Who do we turn to? God! That's who! We trust God! We believe His Word! Please know this does not mean to stop taking your medication. This means we cooperate with The Holy Spirit's leading! We use wisdom with discernment because not all doctors are evil, and not all medicine is bad.

Let's study some scriptures that prove He is our ultimate physician. Look up these scriptures, meditate on them, and ask yourself, where is your belief? Then decree, declare, confess, and agree with God and not mankind.

Proverbs 12:18, Isaiah 58:8, Matthew 25:46, Matthew 4:23, John 6:2

_____

_____

_____

_____

_____

If you have done all you can do. For example, the spiritual disciplines, the elders laid hands, prayed, rested, never doubted, and still healing has not manifested, remember God's sovereignty. He knows what He is doing. Trust Him! He might be teaching you something through this. It might be your current spiritual classroom.

Also, remember that there were strong, faithful believers who remained sick. For example, Paul had a thorn in his flesh and Timothy needed to be disciplined so he wouldn't get sick often.[lxxvii]. Paul even left Trophimus sick.[lxxviii] Friends, our job is to have faith that healing will manifest. It is God's job to manifest that healing; however, He chooses.

---

1 Peter 2:24 (TPT)

[24]He himself carried our sins in His body on the cross so that we would be dead to sin and live for righteousness. Our instant healing flowed from His wounding.

Day Sixteen: Judgment

The lies we sometimes believe:

God is punishing me, so He is sending me His judgment. What will my husband/wife think of me? I will always be rejected, so I will reject others first. I am better than that person. At least I am not like her/him.

The truth that sets us free:

Ephesians 1:3-6 (NIV)

[3]Praise be to the God and Father of our Lord Jesus Christ, who has blessed us in the heavenly realms with every spiritual blessing in Christ. [4]For He chose us in Him before the creation of the world to be holy and blameless in His sight. In Love [5]He predestined us for adoption to Sonship through Jesus Christ, in accordance with His pleasure and will – [6]to the praise of His glorious grace, which He has freely given us in the One He loves.

Replacing the lie with the truth:

God knew before we even entered the stage called earth, what our sins would be. He knew what mistakes we would make. What our thoughts would be. Still, He chose us! Yet, He loves us! Again, He calls us His! He does not judge us with punishment. His love is immense and covers all our sins. He is not an angry God seeking to bring guilt, shame, or condemnation to His Beloved children. Negative judgment is not from His heart. Righteous judgment realigns us back to Him. Let us silence the voice of the enemy and confess the sound of the one true God, Adonai!

Time to Decree, Declare, Confess, and Agree:

In the name of Jesus Christ, I decree, declare, confess, and agree that Jesus Christ paid for the price of all of my sins. His sacrifice on the cross was enough to cover all of my sins. I decree, declare, confess, and agree that God is not sending me unholy judgment.

I decree, declare, confess, and agree that the only opinion that truly matters is the one Jesus Christ has of me. His view is the one I seek. The one I hunger for.

I decree, declare, confess, and agree that I am filled with the fullness of God. Rejection is not in my mind. I do not reject others, nor do others reject me. For I am in the fullness of God.

I decree, declare, confess, and agree that I am fearfully and wonderfully created. There's no need for me to compare to others. When comparison tries to show it's ugly head, I agree with God's word when He says that in my weakness He is strong. In the name of Yeshua HaMashiach I pray, Amen!

Day Sixteen: Reprieve & Relieved

When we judge others or ourselves, we are playing God. We are telling Him that He made a mistake that we can fix. My friends when we judge others, we are placing a mirror on them. We see ourselves in them. Mostly, we see the things we hate about ourselves. That my friend is a ticket to hardships, trials, and many tears.

When we judge, we are also not loving. God calls us to love without restraint. The world lacks love! "And because the world lacks love, there is much hatred, grudge, bitterness, resentment, vengeance, murder, violence, and so many other things that destroy humanity." lxxix

Let's do a 180° and allow God to be God. Look up these scriptures. As you read them, meditate on them and ask The Holy Spirit to break your heart for any judgment you have had for others and yourself. Allow Him to convict you. He is purifying your heart and soul. What is He telling you? If you need more space, use a blank paper.

Psalm 145:8, Isaiah 49:15, Galatians 1:10, John 15:18, Galatians 6:4-5

_____

_____

_____

_____

_____

Day Seventeen: Opposition

The lies we sometimes believe:

This is too hard, so it must not be from God. This resistance proves I am out of God's will.

The truth that sets us free:

Hebrews 13:20-21 (AMP)

[20]Now may the God of peace [the source of serenity and spiritual well-being] who brought up from the dead our Lord Jesus, the great Shepherd of the sheep, through the blood that sealed and ratified the eternal covenant, [21]equip you with every good thing to carry out His will and strengthen you [making you complete and perfect as you ought to be], accomplishing in us that which is pleasing in His sight, through Jesus Christ, to whom be the glory forever and ever. Amen.

Replacing the lie with the truth:

Although there's been much theological debate on who wrote the book of Hebrews, we do know that God's breath was in it. Therefore, we can take it to the bank. My personal opinion is that the Apostle Paul wrote it because he presented the case of Jesus Christ being the One true deity. In the above verses, He, Adonai, is telling us that He is consecrating us for His will. So no matter what we do or how much resistance we experience, we can attest, we are in God's will. He approves us!

In fact, if we encounter resistance, rejoice! Rejoice because God is birthing in you and through you something amazing. Something glorious for His Kingdom. Something that only you can create. Something that will blow your socks off!

To this end, the work that He is birthing in you is going to be so good, so rejoice! Thank Him for the resistance. Thank Him and accept that you are in His will. He will not let go of your hand until your assignment is completed. Trust, lean, and press into Him!

Time to Decree, Declare, Confess, and Agree:

I decree, declare, confess, and agree that Jesus Christ will expose the true motives of my heart to me. Though my heart may deceive me, Jesus Christ will not.

I decree, declare, confess, and agree that everything that is from Holy Spirit will be birth with supernatural peace. When I face opposition, and it is from God, He, Holy Spirit, will give me peace.

I decree, declare, confess, and agree that God gives me the strength, courage, and refreshes my soul with all that I need to carry out my assignment. He brings me the right guidance and advisers.

> Proverbs 24:6 (KJV)
> 6For by wise counsel thou shalt make thy war: and in a multitude of counselors, there is safety.

Day Seventeen: Humility

What does it mean to be a humble person? What is the Biblical definition of a humble person? Well, to define a word in its Biblical meaning, we need to look at what the original authors intended. So we look at the Strong's definitions. "Strong's numbers are an index of every word in the original Hebrew and Greek texts of the Bible.[lxxx]" When we look at Strong's Exhaustive Concordance[lxxxi] #6038. anavah (an-aw-vaw'), the definition of humility is; gentleness and meekness. It comes from the word Strong's #6035. anab (aw-nawv', aw-nawv), which means; poor, afflicted, humble, meek, and lowly.

Again, it is essential to look at the Hebrew and Greek words so we can understand the accurate interpretation. So we can have some girth in our words. And understand what the actual authors were trying to tell us. So now ask yourself, what does your soul (mind, will, emotions, spirit) say to you when you hear; gentleness, meekness, poor, afflicted, and lowly? Would you consider yourself a humble person? A lowly person? A gentle person?

Basically, we are to face opposition with gentleness, meekness, with a lowly perspective. When opposition rise against us, we are to be lowly. We are to serve with a heart of tenderness. We are to serve others as Jesus Christ served them. We are humble servants. Jesus Christ, who had every right to rise against His opposition, served them. He was humble, meek, kind, gentle, poor, and afflicted.

Still, this may be a hard concept to grasp for some because of the pain they have experienced from abusive leaders. Or if your heart is telling you that you are a leader but others don't recognize you. The goal is to serve as Jesus Christ served. Stay humble, stay gentle, and stay lowly.

At times, you may feel their opposition is a disruption to your calling. But your calling was birthed in the belly of your mother. Nothing and no one, except you, can stop the assignment or Ordination, in your life. It is your obedience to The Holy Spirit and your humility that will spiritually promote you.

Besides, remember that Jesus Christ came to serve not to be served. He didn't come to seek titles, He came to rescue. So, when you feel massive opposition from others, that's when we need to evaluate ourselves. Are we ready to lead if we are not ready to follow? If we are serving from a place of humility, the Lord will promote us.

However, if you are serving from a pure heart and still face opposition, remember the Lord's calling in your life. Ask Him to flood you with His love. Ask Him to flood you with His presence until it kills any self-exaltation in you. Ask Him to keep you in the fire. In the pruning. Ask Him to increase so that you can decrease. Ask Him to renew your mind so that you can see clearly from His perspective. Ask Him to show you how to love as He loves. Ask Him to teach you to serve as He served.

In reality, your opposition is a blessing in disguise. It is there to kill that which is inside of you that needs to burn off. It is there to expose the true motives of your heart. It is there to reveal to you what God is still working on. It is there to teach you if you are serious about God or if you are just playing church.

In contrast, there is also a God-given opposition. That's when your spirit (your heart and soul) is trying to stop you from going the wrong way. The closer you get to Jesus Christ, the quicker you will learn to discern if it's opposition from God or for God.

Now, it's time to study some scriptures and renew our minds. Remember to read the scriptures, meditate on the scriptures, digest the scriptures, try to memorize them, write your decrees, declarations, confessions, and agreements with the Word. What do you understand from the scriptures below?

Congratulations! Pat yourself on the back, you are a few days away from killing the 21 lies and agreeing with God's truth.

Psalm 110:4

_____

_____

_____

_____

_____

Hebrews 7:17

_____

_____

_____

_____

_____

Romans 1:6

_____

_____

_____

_____

_____

Romans 11:29

_____

_____

_____

_____

_____

Mark 16:20

_____

_____

_____

_____

_____

Philippians 3:14

_____

_____

_____

_____

_____

Day Eighteen: Pain

The lies we sometimes believe:

It is godly to have pain. True servants experience pain. Pain is a confirmation of my calling. Pain lets me know I am alive. Pain is my gain. Pain is my friend. Pain reminds me to be grateful for what I have.

The truth that sets us free:

John 8:31-32 (KJV)

[31]Then said Jesus to those Jews which believed on Him, If ye continue in my word, then are ye my disciples indeed;

[32]And ye shall know the truth, and the truth shall make you free.

Replacing the lie with the truth:

When we stand on the truth, the truth of God, in God's Word, we kill the belief and the faith in pain. Because we were designed to bring Him, our heavenly Father, pleasure. We were created to bring honor and glory to His name.

Time to Decree, Declare, Confess, and Agree:

I decree, declare, confess, and agree with God's Word that says I was created to please Him. He confirmed my calling in my mother's womb. He gives me the breath to be alive. I agree it is ungodly to accept pain. I decree, declare, confess, and agree that if I keep my mind focused on the work of the Kingdom, I will be a faithful servant of God. I will stand firm on His Word and fight for a pain-free life. His way, not my way. His Spirit, not my flesh.

Day Eighteen: Godly pleasure

There are many Theological teachings out in the world about physical pain and how it is godly (just to be clear, we are not talking about pain from exercise). How suffering and pain produce a devout, humble, and gentler person. You've heard it said over and over, *"pain is a symptom of a fallen world."* Or even *"pain is a symptom of unforgiveness." "A symptom of needed repentance." "A symptom of grief."* These quotes are from various sources of APEST (Apostles, Prophets, Evangelists, Shepherds, & Teachers) leaders that teach the same thing over and over. YouTube and Google are flooded with APEST members telling the congregation to accept their suffering as a gift and a time of consecration to be one on one with God.

However, in Apostle Ryan's Book, he talks about spiritual warfare and how *"if allowed Jezebel will lead a person to a bed of affliction."*[lxxxii] So if you think maybe it's demonic oppression, possession, or affliction, you could be right. After all, this is a fallen world subject to physical manifestations.

Perhaps, as fallen men and women, our brains tell us there's nothing you can do about it. Our minds reconcile with acceptable teachings. Our brains get programmed to accept, welcome, and even embrace the pain.

Yet, God tells us to study His word because, in His Word, we will find the truth. The truth that says we please Him; see Isaiah 43:7. He created us to be children in His garden roaming free. His Word will make us free. Free from the belief that we are to embrace the pain.

Contrary to popular belief, pain is not our friend. Pain keeps you from experiencing all that your creator has for you. He has a lot of work for you in His Kingdom and has given you many tools to defeat pain.

To illustrate, when you have done all that you can do. Like, practicing the spiritual disciplines to heal your soul. Cooperated with The Holy Spirit on your lifestyle. United with The Holy Spirit on your diet. Worked with The Holy Spirit and your physician or natural path. And you have not had a breakthrough, ask yourself, do I believing I am in Adam (fallen man) or am I in Christ (resurrected and alive). Because Christ did not embrace the pain. He knew the schemes of the enemy. Jesus Christ silenced the voice of the enemy with scripture. Over and over, He repeated, "For it is written."

So, let us boldly follow the teachings of Jesus Christ and allow Him to live in us. Faithful servants believe that Jesus Christ suffered pain at the cross but did not embrace it. Because of the sacrifice on the cross, we cannot think it is godly to have pain. We must rebuke it and cast it to the abyss.

Now it's time for you to reconcile with God. Forgive the Lord, your God. Forgive Him for not intervening when you thought He should. Forgive Him for not intervening when bad things happened. Forgive Him for the moments you have felt disillusioned. Forgive Him for the times you thought He was not there. Forgive Him for not healing you when you thought He should. It's time to forgive God.

Friends, it is okay to forgive God. He's a big boy, He can take it. Plus, it will bring you such a spiritual relief that you can't imagine. He loves you so much! He doesn't need your forgiveness, but forgiving Him is for you. So how do you forgive God? Let's follow His steps.

Look up the following verses. After you have read them, allows yourself to forgive God. You are learning to bring down the wall that stands between you and Him. Don't give the enemy any more foothold, release forgiveness! Set your soul free! What do the scriptures say about forgiving? Can you use these scriptures to forgive God? Write to Him. Let Him know you have forgiven Him. If you need additional paper, just use a blank page.

Luke 6:37, Romans 12:17-18, Job 30:21, Ephesians 4:26

_____

_____

_____

_____

_____

_____

_____

_____

Dear beloved ones, the price of unforgiveness is impotence. We are impotent against the pain that binds us. Through forgiveness, unforgiveness is broken. The cost of forgiveness is freedom. As a result of freedom, we exude power and emit the righteousness of Jesus Christ in us. We exude royalty.

Please note, you can't set yourself free. Only through the leading of The Holy Spirit can you be free. Allow Him to work in and through you. Forgiveness will unbind you and release you into authentic godly pleasures.

Day Nineteen: Past

The lies we sometimes believe:

I am who I am, I will never change. I'm too burned by my past. I will always be recovering from XYZ. If they only knew who I was. What I've done and where I've been. If they only knew!

The truth that sets us free:

Philippians 3:13-14 (TPT)

[13]I don't depend on my own strength to accomplish this; however, I do have one compelling focus: I forget all of the past as I fasten my heart to the future instead. [14]I run straight for the divine invitation of reaching the heavenly goal and gaining the victory prize through the anointing of Jesus.

Replacing the lie with the truth:

I am not my past! Like the Apostle Paul, I pursued my ambitions, but today I am a new creation. No longer a Pharisee but a Son/Daughter of the Highest.

Time to Decree, Declare, Confess, and Agree:

I decree, declare, confess, and agree that Yâhh, the true God, is giving me a new heart. Removing my heart of stone and giving me a heart of flesh.[lxxxiii] I decree, declare, confess, and agree that there is no longer any damnation in my future. I decree, declare, confess, and agree that Yâhh is birthing in me full restoration. I am made whole. I decree, declare, confess, and agree that I do not lie to my brethren. He's taken off my old self. I now walk-in full transparency.[lxxxiv]

Day Nineteen: Divinely Created Future

The Apostle Paul, who was the crème de la crème of the Hebrews, stated that he had flaws. He lets us know that he was not perfect, made mistakes, and had a past. After all, he was part of the crowd who stoned Stephen. Remember, he, Saul, who later became Paul, watched over the coats of the people who were stoning Stephen and approved their actions.[lxxxv] He watched as they stoned Stephen to death! The Passion Translation version goes on to add that Stephen's death was the initiation of Saul. Stephen, the first martyr, and Saul, who was divinely created into Paul, met grace that evening.

Since he was part of the first persecution of the church. So, of course, he would be the perfect example of how we need to deal with our past. He's one of our spiritual leaders and ensures us, he's forward focus. He sees the end line, sees the goal, and he is not looking back.

Thus, straight-ahead, we must push past the past and focus on the heavenly prize. Let us take a note from our teacher – Apostle Paul and be forward thinkers. Heal your past by focusing on your spiritual race. Your spiritual race. Not someone else. See, that's a trap of the enemy called comparison. When we start to compare our lane with another's, we begin to feel frustrated and think we will never change. Let's not take that bait. Like Paul, you have a unique spiritual assignment specifically tailored for you.

For this purpose, let us study the following Bible verses. As you read the scriptures, ask The Holy Spirit to speak to you and show you your spiritual race. Ask The Holy Spirit, why you are here, and where are you going. Write down what He tells you.

Romans 12:2 (TPT) [2]Stop imitating the ideals and opinions of the culture around you, but be inwardly transformed by The Holy Spirit through a total reformation of how you think. This will empower you to discern God's will as you live a beautiful life, satisfying and perfect in His eyes.

_____

_____

_____

_____

_____

_____

Ephesians 4:23 (AMP) [23]and be continually renewed in the spirit of your mind [having a fresh, untarnished mental and spiritual attitude],

_____

_____

_____

_____

1 John 2:15 – 17 (TPT) [15]Don't set the affections of your heart on this world or in loving the things of the world. The love of the Father and the love of the world are incompatible. [16]For all that the world can offer us – the gratification of our flesh, the allurement of the things of the world, and the obsession with status and importance – none of these things come from the Father but from the world. [17]This world and its desires are in the process of passing away, but those who love to do the will of God will live forever.

_____

_____

_____

_____

_____

_____

1 Peter 2:21-22 (AMP) [21]For [as a believer] you have been called for this purpose, since Christ suffered for you, leaving you an example, so that you may follow in His footsteps. [22]HE COMMITTED NO SIN, NOR WAS DECEIT EVER FOUND IN HIS MOUTH.

_____

_____

_____

_____

Although change only happens when a person is ready to die to their selves, there is a spiritual road map to experience a complete transformation. A full turn around in their lives. This topic is near and dear to my heart because if I can now live a righteous life, so can you.

For instance, some people like myself started attending Celebrate Recovery[lxxxvi]. The pain from my past was so bad that I could not allow God or anyone else to help me. I refused to listen to The Holy Spirit. So God created a step by step plan for people like me too hurt to submit. The lies I believed kept taking an ax to my faith. I was angry at God but didn't know it. There was so much pain and numbness in my life. I was like a wounded animal. Full of rage and anger, "beneath the pain or numbness lies a force that wants to lash out and hurt the thing that hurt us-an animal reflex anger."[lxxxvii] Celebrate Recovery taught me to submit to calm the animal within me. To ease the raging storm.

Another great tool that I have personally experienced is having a Sozo.[lxxxviii] In a short summary, a Sozo is a healing and deliverance session that gets to the root of a problem. A healing and deliverance session must take place so that your soul can begin to transform. Contact your local church for private sessions.

In like manner, Biblical Counseling. "A Biblical counselor is simply a faithful teacher and brother or sister in Christ."[lxxxix] It's like ministering. You come alongside a brother or sister in the faith. walking with them through life. Teaching scriptures that apply to life's challenges. At times it is rebuking the wrong thinking with love. It is about loving them where they are and helping them find the truth in scripture. Like this book. It reveals the lies of the enemy. It shows you scriptures to combat them.

Not only is Biblical Counseling needed, but in combination with Biblical Life Coaching, it provides a knock-out punch to the enemy of your soul. Biblical Life Coaching, as described by Dr. Gary Collins, is "the art and practice of guiding a person or group from where they are toward the greater competence and fulfillment that they desire."[xc] Meaning, the coachee is in charge of their path. The Biblical Life Coach is here to help them grow but not necessarily heal. However, we are always led by The Holy Spirit.

Celebrate Recovery, Sozo's, healing, deliverance, Biblical Counseling, Biblical Life Coaching, and the spiritual disciplines are great tools to begin a life transformation. But all of that wed with serving and tithing is what will manifest real permanent transformation. It all starts with a willing heart. A heart that is ready to submit. A heart that has had enough of doing it their way.

Concurrently, Holy Spirit is your ultimate teacher and your guide. He will show you the road map. He will show you where you are in your spiritual walk and what the next step will be. Just ask Him to show you. Remember, everyone has a different road map. So don't stress if one thing doesn't work out for you. Keep pressing, keep being obedient, keep listening. And NEVER compare yourself to another believer!

In like manner, the deeper you go with this study, the more transformation you will experience. The outcome will be based on how much you connected with Jesus Christ, The Holy Spirit, and

Father God. It is a process that **you** must go through. It will be painful, but if you genuinely desire to change, it will be so worth it. I am a living testimony of Yâhh's (God) transformation power. He pulled me from the muck and the mire and forever changed me. Now I get to testify! So, how badly do you want your life to change? Are you tired of the same o', same o'? Have you had enough?

Above all, remember that He is faithful. He will complete the work that you allow Him to do. He gave you free will. He will honor it and will enable you to choose. Just like Adam and Eve did. So, let us continue with some verses. Remember, dig deep. Really meditate, marinate, chew, and look for the marrow on these verses. What do they say to you? Write out decree's, declaration's, confession's, and agreement's with the Word.

Philippians 1:6 (TPT) ⁶I pray with great faith for you, because I'm fully convinced that the One who began this glorious work in you will faithfully continue the process of maturing you and will put His finishing touches to it until the unveiling of our Lord Jesus Christ.

_____

_____

_____

_____

_____

_____

Proverbs 9:10 (AMP) ¹⁰The [reverent] fear of the Lord [that is, worshiping Him and regarding Him as truly awesome] is the beginning and the preeminent part of wisdom [its starting point and its essence], And the knowledge of the Holy One is understanding and spiritual insight.

_____

_____

_____

_____

_____

1 Corinthians 10:13 (AMP)

13No temptation [regardless of its source] has overtaken or enticed you that is not common to human experience [nor is any temptation unusual or beyond human resistance];

but God

is faithful [to His word-He is compassionate and trustworthy], and He will not let you be tempted beyond your ability [to resist], but along with the temptation He [has in the past and is now and] will [always] provide the way out as well, so that you will be able to endure it [without yielding, and will overcome temptation with joy].

Day Twenty: Separation

The lies we sometimes believe:

It is okay to be lonely. People won't even remember me. They don't like me. I'd rather be alone than to be hurt again. I'm in my quiet space with the Lord. Isolation is better for me. I don't have to attend a corporate "church" service. I prefer to connect through social media only.

The truth that sets us free:

Hebrews 10:25 (NIV)

[25]not giving up meeting together, as some are in the habit of doing, but encouraging one another-and all the more as you see the Day approaching.

Replacing the lie with the truth:

When we continue to meet with other like-minded believers, we encourage each other, we uplift each other, and we strengthen each other. When we walk through life by ourselves, we can get caught up in our despair and think we have no value.

To add, social media can be a great tool to reach the masses. During the Pandemic, it was the only source of connection for some people. But a genuine connection happens face to face. When we walk with others, we see we add value to their lives. We all need each other to grow stronger and stronger for the day of Jesus Christ's return.

Time to Decree, Declare, Confess, and Agree:

I decree, declare, confess, and agree that Jesus Christ is my friend. I am never lonely because He is always with me. He sees everything I do and watches over everything I say. He is in my thoughts and searches my heart for His presence. I decree, declare, confess, and agree that I will be remembered as a blessing and not a burden. I decree, declare, confess, and agree that I fellowship with like-minded people. I decree, declare, confess, and agree that I practice safe boundaries. I, through the grace of God, have learned to trust again. I decree that I will not use time with the Lord as an excuse for hiding from life. I decree, declare, confess, and agree that iron sharpens iron.[xci] Therefore, isolation is a trick from the enemy to make me a weak person. I agree with God's Word that says I was created to fellowship.[xcii]

Day Twenty: Orchestrated Unification

It is never okay to be lonely or isolated. Let's read the Merriam-Webster's definition of lonely: "2: not frequented by human beings: desolate."[xciii] And what does desolate mean: joyless, sorrowful, separation from a loved one.[xciv] Separation, do you hear that it means we are cut off from the body. The body that flows the Blood of Jesus Christ. He made us the body. A comprehensive unit.

---

1 Corinthians 12:12-14 (KJV)

[12]For as the body is one, and hath many members, and all the members of that one body, being many, are one body: so also is Christ.
[13]For by one Spirit are we all baptized into one body, whether we be Jews or Gentiles, whether we be bond or free; and have been all made to drink into one Spirit.
[14]For the body is not one member, but many.

He created you to minister to me and me to minister to you. He knew we were going to need each other. Even Jesus Christ needed help carrying His cross. Loneliness and isolation are lies from the pit of hell to keep us bound in a joyless life. People need you, you have a unique gift inside of you. Something exceptional that no one else has. Something that brings a smile to someone else. Plus, trusting people again takes time. It means setting healthy boundaries. It means walking in transparency. Because, my friend, people need to see the real you, warts and all. They need to see you without your make up. They need to see you when you are happy and when you are sad. An authentic transparent you will be inviting to authentic, transparent people.

To this end, let's pause for a second and talk about the so-called Sunday worship. Often you will hear scripture being used to testify to "Sunday Service, Sunday Worship or the Lord's day" as a means to fellowship **only** on that day. Let me repeat that again "only" on Sunday. Meaning to fellowship only on "church" day.

For example, in Genesis 2:2, the words used are "Seventh Day." However, when we look at the Strong's definition of "Seventh Day," used in Genesis 2:2, we find "Shabath.[xcv]" You will not find "Sunday Service, Sunday Worship, or the Lord's day".

Further, some churches use "The Lord's Day" as a foundation for Sunday Service. The scriptures to back that up are; Acts 20:7 and Revelation 1:10[xcvi]. You can dive a little deeper into that opinion at blueletterbible.org/faq/sabbath.cfm. There's a great website that talks about the Sabbath. You can visit them at your leisure: https://www.sabbathtruth.com/

My understanding, from Yâhh, scriptures, teachings, and sermons, is that Saturday is the true Sabbath. That the Apostles fellowshipped "daily." Still, I have up to the writing of this book, yet to find a church that does service on Saturday.

Which brings me to the next point, attending "corporate church service." Is it for today? Absolutely, you need to be around people. They need to be around you. It's harmful to be isolated. It's unhealthy to be lonely. Remember, it kills your joy. So, yes, get out of your home and into a church service. Even if it is a Sunday service. <wink>

Also, streaming is a great way to watch service when you can't physically attend but make every effort to get out of the house and into a church. The rays from the sun will produce endorphins in your body. These endorphins are the happy-serotonin that you need to break from isolation.

Now, it's time for you to put what you have learned into practice. Let's study some scriptures. What does the Lord want to reveal to you through them? What do you sense the Lord telling you through these scriptures?

Luke 6:31

_____

_____

_____

_____

_____

Proverbs 19:20

_____

_____

_____

_____

_____

_____

_____

Ecclesiastes 4:9-10

_____

_____

_____

_____

_____

_____

1 Corinthians 3:10

_____

_____

_____

_____

_____

_____

Hebrews 3:13

_____

_____

_____

_____

_____

_____

Day Twenty-One: Shame

The lies we sometimes believe:

I deserved this humiliation. I need to keep my head bowed. I am broken; therefore, I am unworthy of being loved. I don't belong anywhere. I have not confessed all my sins, there must be more. What is wrong with me? I just want to crawl into a hole and hide!

The truth that sets us free:

1 John 1:9 (AMP)

⁹If we [freely] admit that we have sinned and confess our sins, He is faithful and just [true to His own nature and promises], and will forgive our sins and cleanse us continually from all unrighteousness [our wrongdoing, everything not in conformity with His will and purpose].

Replacing the lie with the truth:

Shame gives us unholy guilt and condemnation. It is the voice of the enemy of your soul It makes us think we deserved to be humiliated, in bondage, enslaved, ridiculed, and or cast out. The lie of the enemy keeps many in bondage without knowing that the antidote is just a confession away. Not a confession to a Catholic Priest but a verbal admission to a trustworthy person. If you don't have an honest person, confess to The Holy Spirit. He'll help you and guide you.

As a matter of fact, Apostle John tells us all we have to do is by faith, confess to Jesus Christ. Confess to him whatever sin we have committed. We are not to live in the synagogues and keep confessing over and over again like a religious Pharisee. No! Now, we confess to Jesus Christ and leave it. We ask Him for forgiveness and receive by faith, His mercy. Everything we do and say is by faith.

Additionally, when He forgives us, He, because of His love, also washes us. He cleanses us. He purifies us. He makes us right. Thereby, we learn to be right. We grasp we are made right, righteously. We discover we are in right standing with God. We are righteous.

Time to Decree, Declare, Confess, and Agree:

I decree, declare, confess, and agree that I am the light of this world. My Heavenly Father Loves me. Humiliation is not of Him.

I decree, declare, confess, and agree that God upholds me when I feel broken. He, Abba, heals my broken heart and binds up my wounds.

I decree, declare, confess, and agree that God thinks I am precious and honored before His sight. He loves me so much, He will give up people and nations just for me. I decree, declare, confess, and agree I am of Royal Blood!

Day Twenty-One: He, God, Approves You!

It's hard to understand in our western world about Royalty. We don't have Kings or Queens, so we can't see what it looks like to live a life of Royalty. Nonetheless, that's what God says we are. WE ARE ROYALTY! We are Royalty! Let that sink in. Let it sink deep into your marrow. Down in your belly. YOU ARE OF ROYAL BLOOD! You, yes, you have a crown over your head. YOU are Royalty!

As we wrap up the last day of our study, I wanted us to focus on that topic. We are Royalty! Scream it at the top of your lungs. WE ARE ROYALTY! Scream it, my friend; I AM ROYALTY! We have defeated the 21 lies of the enemy of our souls and have settled into our true identity, we're Royalty! Kathryn Kuhlman understood very clearly she was Royalty. "Everything Kathryn did was big. When she preached, even if there were only a handful of people in the building, she preached like there were ten thousand."[xcvii]

Now, let's put that into practice. Let's get some meat in our Bible bones. Look up these scriptures. After you have read them. Write a decree, along with a declaration, confess you agree with them, and allow Holy Spirit to work the Word (scripture) in you.

1 Peter 2:9

Proverbs 25:2

Mark 4:11

Romans 8:15-17

_____

_____

_____

_____

_____

Revelation 5:10

_____

_____

_____

_____

1 Peter 3:3-4

_____

_____

_____

_____

_____

Romans 8:17

_____

_____

_____

_____

_____

Do you understand now that you are REMARKABLE? Do you know that you are loved? Do you know that you were wholly created? Nothing in this world matters more to God than you! He watches over you, and He cares for you. He waits for you to open your eyes in the morning, and He waits to hear you speak. He calls you His! His perfect, beautiful, Royal son and Royal daughter. He loves you with a love that lasts forever, an everlasting love.

Section Three: In Conclusion

So I will restore to you the years that the
swarming locust has eaten, the crawling locust,
the consuming locust, and the chewing locust, My
great army which I sent among you.

Joel 2:25-26 (NKJV)

The Bible, this study, the Bible, sermons, and the spiritual disciplines will mean nothing to you if you have no faith. Faith is our God-given currency. It is a Father's inheritance to His children.

According to Merriam-Webster's Online Dictionary, the word faith[xcviii] is described as:

Noun:
1. a: allegiance to duty or a person: Loyalty
    b (1): fidelity to one's promises
    (2): sincerity of intentions

2. a (1): belief and trust in and loyalty to God.
    (2): belief in the traditional doctrines of a religion
    b (1): firm belief in something for which there is no proof.
    (2): complete trust

3.: something that is believed especially with strong conviction
    especially: a system of religious beliefs
    on faith: without question

Verb:
    faithed; faithing; faiths

Transitive verb
    archaic: believe, trust

► Based on this definition, do you have faith? ◄

> ## Romans 10:17 (AMP)
>
> [17]So faith comes from hearing [what is told], and what is heard comes by the [preaching of the] message concerning Christ.

In the same way, according to scripture, faith comes to our ears from what our mouths say. The words that we speak with our mouths pierce our ears and penetrate our hearts. Our hearts inevitably transform.

In other words, your heart transformation will come from the inside out. You will begin to have a softer heart. A brighter outlook on life. The more you dedicate your life to studying the Word of God, the more your inside will become your outside.

As a result of this, people around you will notice the faith you have. They will be drawn to it. But, brace yourself because it's a process. **Change won't happen overnight.** So, be gracious to yourself. Be kind to God. Let Him pierce your heart with His Word. Let Him show you how to cash in your faith currency. He's your Father and all He wants to do is talk to you. Your faith is that conduit He's looking for.

Nonetheless, if you have no faith, just ask Him to fill you with it. Ask Him to help you have a full faith bank account. He's your loving Daddy who wants to provide, love, protect, bless, give you freedom, security, and cherish you! He calls you His! He wants to shower you with all kinds of goodness. He wants you to know you are valued, treasured, adorned with righteousness, and fearfully made. He withholds nothing from you. Just bathe in His goodness, His rest, and His provision. Allow Him to love you and allow yourself to love Him back.

Thank you for going on this journey with me as we kill the 21 lies of the enemy of your soul, decree, declare, confess, and agree with the Word of God over them. I ask Yâhh to bless you immensely!

Now go and be a blessing to someone else. Show them the lies of the enemy of humankind and teach them to kill the lies. Teach them the Word of Yâhh (God), to live boundlessly, and to be Royalty! Teach them to rest in the truth of His unfailing Word. Teach them to be in the overflow of His goodness, mercy, and grace.

Remember, without stepping out in faith,
it is impossible to see
the manifested hand of God move.

It won't be easy to change your mindset.
It might take a while
but press in. It will be so worth it.

You are only one fear away from seeing His face and
His hands in your situation.

Face your fear in faith so that He can move.

Don't limit Him!

Don't limit your faith in Him!
Trust Him!

May you know without a shadow of a doubt that you
are loved and prayed for.

~ Coach Yolanda Nichols

Quick Definitions

The following are quick definitions of the words used in this study and then some. For a thorough description, please see the end-notes.

Kabod[xcix]: The Glory of God; the heavy feeling of His presence within you; sensing, feeling, seeing, smelling, touching, and hearing God's limitless presence. The human body's reaction to God's Omnipotent Presence.

Decree[c]: Notification, bringing awareness, attention, dictate, warrant served.

Declare[ci]: Kingdom Seal, authority seal, official guarantee, warrant processed.

Success[cii]: Outgrowing; a current circumstance, beliefs, patterns, and cycles; aka breaking through or birthing, a permanent change in the mind.

Sanctified[ciii]: Set apart for Abba; made holy; encapsulated for Abba. To be bubbled by God for His purpose.

Offense[civ]: The bait, hook, or switch that the enemy of humankind, aka satan, uses to manipulate people.

Authority[cv]: Your power, your right, and your responsibility.

Sheol[cvi]: Hell, the place of eternal torment. Created to bind the enemy of humankind forever.

Righteousness[cvii]: Standing upright before God.

Triune Man: Body, Soul, Spirit: 1st Thessalonians 5:23, Hebrews 4:12

Names Of God Used In This Study

1. Abba[cviii]:   The Hebrew name for God; closes definition is Father; phonetics: äb-bä.[cix]

2. YHWH[cx]:   Known as the Tetragrammaton. It is the personal name of God in Hebrew. Out of respect, it is not pronounced. Closes pronunciation according to Strong's is Yĕhovah; phonetics: yeh·hō·vä'.[cxi]

3. Elohim[cxii]:   God of gods; the Mighty One; phonetics: el·ō·hēm.[cxiii]

4. Adonai[cxiv]:   Hebrew name of God signifying Lord; phonetics: ad·ō·nōy.[cxv]

5. Kyrios[cxvi]:   Lord or Master; Supreme Authority; phonetics: kü'-rē-os.[cxvii]

6. Jehovah Rapha:
   Healer; "The Lord Your Healer."[cxviii]

6. Yâhh[cxix]   The proper name of the one true God; the sacred name; phonetics: yä.[cxx]

7. God: The God of the Hebrews; the God of Moses, Isaac, Jacob, and the Apostle Paul

8. Holy Spirit: He is the 3rd person of the Godhead. He is the Ruach[cxxi] (phonetics: rü'·akh[cxxii]) or Spirit of the Godhead. The word "Spirit often means the spiritual presence, power, or nature of Yeshua;[cxxiii] Also known as the Holy Ghost.

9. Jesus Christ:
   The Son of God and the son of mankind. He is the only way, the truth, and the life.[cxxiv] He is the door to our Father; phonetics: DZHEE-SUHS[cxxv]

10. Yeshua HaMashiach:
   Hebrew name for "Jesus the Messiah."[cxxvi] meaning the anointed one.

Please note that this is not a comprehensive list of names used for God, our Savior Jesus Christ, and The Holy Spirit. It is a list of names we used for this study. For a full list of names, you can always do an online search or look up various books on this topic.

Every name given by God has a meaning and a purpose. To have a better relationship with God, we need to study His names, but that's a topic for another time.

In this study, we focused on exposing the lies of the enemy of our soul. Decreeing, declaring, confessing, and agreeing with the truth, which is God's Word over the lies. We got rid of our wrong thinking and aligned our thoughts, feelings, actions, and motives with God's Word. We received some inner healing. We stretched our patters of believe.

Moving forward, we're going to look at things the way He wants us to look at them. We will bypass our natural way of seeing. Instead we will look at things from an eternal perspective. A God-given perspective. The Word is our filter, and the Word is God.

Honoring Each Bible Copyright

1. King James Version (KJV): Scriptures marked KJV are taken from the King James Version (KJV): KING JAMES VERSION, public domain.

2. New King James Version® (NKJV): Scriptures taken from the New King James Version®. Copyright© 1982 by Thomas Nelson. Used by permission. All rights reserved.

3. NIV: Scriptures marked NIV are taken from the NEW INTERNATIONAL VERSION® Copyright© 1973, 1974, 1984, 2011 by Biblica, Inc™. Used by permission of Zondervan.

4. MSG: Scriptures are taken from The Message Bible. Copyright©1993, 1994, 1995, 1996, 2000, 2001, 2002. Used by permission of NavPress Publishing Group.

5. HCSB: Scriptures marked HCSB are taken from the HOLMAN CHRISTIAN STANDARD BIBLE (HCSB): Scripture taken from the HOLMAN CHRISTIAN STANDARD BIBLE, Copyright© 1999, 2000, 2002, 2003 by Holman Bible Publishers, Nashville Tennessee, All rights reserved.

6. AMP: Scriptures marked AMP are taken from the AMPLIFIED BIBLE (AMP): Scripture taken from the AMPLIFIED® BIBLE, Copyright© 1954, 1958, 1962, 1964, 1965, 1987, by the Lockman Foundation Used by Permission. www.Lockman.org

7. TPT: Scripture quotations marked TPT are from The Passion Translation®, Copyright© 2017, 2018 by Passion & Fire Ministries, Inc. Used by permission. All rights reserved. ThePassionTranslation.com

It is important to note that all Bible versions are written by mankind but breathed and inspired by The Holy Spirit. Before discarding any Bible verse because of the translation, cross-reference with other versions to get the full interpretation. Always be led by The Holy Spirit Himself.

Dedications

1. First of all, to my Lord Jesus Christ. I love you so much! This book is for you, to bring **YOU ALL the honor and ALL the glory**. Holy Spirit, thank you for breathing it. Abba, my Daddy, thank you!

2. To my mother in law, Mrs. Dorothy: Thank you for showing me mercy, grace, forgiveness, and love. You are a true mother!

3. To my mother: Yolanda, te quiero mucho mamá! Gracias por darme vida. Sé que hiciste lo mejor que pudiste.

4. To my hero and my husband: Raymond Nichols, whom I could not have finished it without his support, encouragement, and dedication. Honey, I love you and I respect you more each day. You are a loving husband, a nurturing father, and an example of Christ to all.

5. To my children: Anabel, Melissa, Jesus, Luisito, and my children in heaven. I love you all so much, and I am always very proud of you. We will spend eternity in heaven.

6. To my current and future grandchildren: Julie, Ella, and Luke. May you continue the legacy of serving Jesus Christ and His Kingdom. Blessings to my future grandchildren, Abuela loves you all.

7. To my son in love: Frank; may you continue to be a godly man, a man of honor, and hungry for the heart of Jesus Christ. May you always know that I love you and am very proud of you.

8. To my future daughters-in-love: I am already praying for you, sweethearts.

9. To my siblings, nieces, nephews, brother-in-love, and sister-in-love, may you know without a shadow of a doubt that you can create a new legacy for you and yours.

10. To the countless friends who have taught me the power of unconditional love, unconditional forgiveness, and acceptance, thank you!

11. To the myriad of mentors, both directly and or indirectly that have taught me to live and think differently. This is possible because of you.

Acknowledgments

Without the leading of The Holy Spirit, this book would not exist. It is His timing. It is His breath throughout the book. It is His message. The Holy Spirit is my friend, comforter, and guide. He wants to be yours too.

Furthermore, Abba delights in our obedience to His instructions. He set the example for us when He spoke life into existence. In Genesis 1:3 (KJV) [3]"And God said, Let there be light, and there was light." Light is life. He "spoke" and created life. You, like Him, can create. He wants us to use the power of our tongue to create His desires. We can use it to bless others or we can use it to speak death to others. Which one do you choose? Blessings or death? God wants you to actively speak or make daily declarations, decrees, confessions, and agreements into your life. So, open your mouth and take your power back from the enemy of your soul.

I would also like to acknowledge the countless mentors who breathed life into me. Either through face to face contact, social media, and or other forms of media, thank you! Your spiritual sowing into me has made this book possible. Please keep sowing your gifts. I promise to give everything I have learned back.

In conclusion, when we open our hands and release what we have been given, we get refilled from The Holy Spirit. Friends, we don't hoard gifts, we free them. We publish His treasures.

About the Author

Yolanda Nichols, at the time of this writing, lives in Sunny Arizona with her youngest child and her husband. She is the founder of Yoly's Resource Ministry: serving the disenfranchised; Yolanda Nichols' Training and Discipleship Academy: training and equipping generations; Yoly's Adventure: empowering the entrepreneur; Yoly's Corner: a political-social media platform.

A home-educating mom, Ordained Minister, Coach, and Coach Trainer, Credentialed in Basic Biblical Life Coaching, Credentialed in Advanced Transformational Life Coaching, Credentialed in Ministry Building: Mantle of God, Certified as Advanced Master Mentor, Certified as Marriage Mentor and Relationship Coach, Certified KIMI Power Club, Certified as a Secular Life Coach, Certified as a Counselling Practitioner (Beginner to Advance), an entrepreneur, and an author.

Yet, her greatest achievement is discovering she is the daughter of the King of Kings. Now she teaches others to live out John 10:10 overflow.

End Notes-

May you be blessed by His richness.

i ► 2 Corinthians 5:7 Amplified Version (AMP) 7 for we walk by faith, not by sight [living our lives in a manner consistent with our confident belief in God's promises.]-

ii ► Ezekiel 34:11 (HCSB) 11 "For this is what the Lord God says: See, I Myself will search for My flock and look for them.

iii ► Psalm 132:13 (TPT) 13 Lord, you have chosen Zion as your dwelling place, for your pleasure is fulfilled in making it your home.

iv ► Psalm 139:14 (NIV) 14 I praise you because I am fearfully and wonderfully made; your works are wonderful, I know that full well.

v ► Heretical: 1. of or relating to adherence to a religious opinion contrary to church dogma: characterized by heresy. 2. or, relating to, or characterized by departure from accepted beliefs or standards: unorthodox.
https://www.merriam-webster.com/dictionary/heretical, Accessed 14, 2019.

vi ► Paraphrased from Psalm 4:3 (NIV) 3 Know that the Lord has set apart his faithful servant for Himself; the Lord hears when I call Him.

vii ► Acts 16:31 (NIV) 31 They replied, "Believe in the Lord Jesus, and you will be saved- you and your household."

viii ► One person's submission does not save another. Still, one person firmly standing in faith for another does move God's hand for their salvation.

ix ► Though the template might change due to advances in technology, the principle will stay the same. Your "New Birth" will be celebrated.

x ► John 15:16bc (KJV) ¹⁶ that ye should go and bring forth fruit, and that your fruit should remain..

xi►Decrees"Hhttps://www.biblestudytools.com/dictionaries/bakers-evangelical-dictionary/decrees.html, Accessed 31 Jan 2018.

xii ► Lack ⊦ Merriam-Webster.com: https://www.merriam-webster.com/dictionary/lack, Accessed 01 Jan 2018.

xiii►Ekklesia⊦ The NAS New Testament Greek Lexicon:
https://www.biblestudytools.com/lexicons/greek/nas/ekklesia.html, Accessed 06 Sep 2018.

► Mark 3:13 (NIV) ¹³ Jesus went up on a mountainside and called to Him those He wanted, and they came to Him.

xiv ► Confession ⊦ 1. a: an act of confessing, 2. b: a formal statement of religious beliefs: CREED, 3: an organized religious body having a common creed.
https://www.merriam-webster.com/dictionary/confession, Accessed 21 Sep 2018.

xv ► Soul ⊦ https://www.collinsdictionary.com/us/dictionary/english/soul, Accessed 21 Sep 2018.

xvi ► Agree ⊦ transitive verb 1a: to concur in (something, such as an opinion) : Admit, Concede b: to consent to as a course of action.
https://www.merriam-webster.com/dictionary/agree, Accessed 04 Nov 2018.

xvii ► John 10.35 I https://biblehub.com/commentaries/john/10_35.htm, Accessed 30 Dec 2018.

xviii ► Genesis 1:28 (AMP) 28 And God blessed them [granting them certain authority] and said to them, "Be fruitful, multiply, and fill the earth, and subjugate it [putting it under your power]; and rule over (dominate) the fish of the sea, the birds of the air, and every living thing that moves upon the earth."

xix ► 1 Corinthians 1:30 (NIV) 30 It is because of Him that you are in Christ Jesus, who has become for us wisdom from God-that is, our righteousness, holiness, and redemption.

xx ► 1 Corinthians 2:16c (NIV) 16 but we have the mind of Christ.

xxi ► 2 Timothy 3:16 (KJV) 16 All scripture is given by inspiration of God, and is profitable for doctrine, for reproof, for correction, for instruction in righteousness:

xxii ► Psalm 84 1-2 (NIV) 1 How lovely is your dwelling place, Lord Almighty! 2 My soul years, even faints, for the courts of the Lord; my heart and my flesh cry out for the living God.

xxiii ►Mark 1:27 (KJV) 27 And they were all amazed, insomuch that they questioned among themselves, saying, What thing is this? What new doctrine is this? For with authority commandeth HE even the unclean spirits, and they do obey Him.

xxiv ► The true Holy Spirit will always: 1. Point to Jesus Christ: see John 4:2-3, 2. Oppose the works of darkness: see Matthew 25:41, 3. Points people to scriptures: see 1 John 4:6, 4. Points people to love Yâhh (God) and love others: see Matthew 22:36-10

xxv ► "The New-Psycho-Cybernetics: Maxwell Maltz, Dan S. Kennedy":
www.amazon.com/New-Psycho-Cybernetics-Maxwell-Maltz/dp/0735202850/, Accessed 31 Jan 2018.

xxvi ► Manifest: 1. readily perceived by the senses and especially by the sense of sight. 2 easily understood or recognized by the mind.
https://www.merriam-webster.com/dictionary/manifest, Accessed, 14 June 2019.

xxvii ► Genesis 12:2 (NIV) 2 "I will make you into a great nation, and I will bless you; I will make your name great, and you will be a blessing.

xxviii ► Luke 21:15 (AMP) 15 for I will give you [skillful] words and wisdom which none of your opponents will be able to resist or refute.

xxix ► Psalm 78:49 (NKJV) 49 He cast on them the fierceness of His anger, Wrath, indignation, and trouble, By sending angels of destruction among them.

xxx ► Acts 16:31 (TPT) 31 They answered, "Believe in the Lord Jesus and you will be saved-you and all your family.

xxxi ► Galatians 6:8 (NKJV) 8 For he who sows to his flesh will of the flesh reap corruption, but he who sows to the Spirit will of the Spirit reap everlasting life.

xxxii ► Hebrews 7:25 (NIV) 25 Therefore He is able to save completely those who come to God through Him, because He always lives to intercede for them.

xxxiii ► Romans 2:4 (AMP) 4 Or do you have no regard for the wealth of His kindness and tolerance and patience [in withholding His wrath]? Are you [actually] unaware or ignorant [of the fact] that God's kindness leads you to repentance [that is, to change your inner self, your old way of thinking-seek His purpose for your life]?

xxxiv ► Deuteronomy 6:12 (KJV) 12 Then beware lest thou forget the Lord, which brought thee forth out of the land of Egypt, from the house of bondage.

xxxv ► Job 1:6 (KJV) 6 Now there was a day when the sons of God came to present themselves before the Lord, and Satan came also among them.

xxxvi ► Matthew 4:1 (NIV) 1 Then Jesus was led by the Spirit into the wilderness to be tempted by the devil.

xxxvii ► Isaiah 14: 12 (NKJV) 12 "How you are fallen from heaven, O Lucifer, son of the morning! How you are cut down to the ground, You who weakened the nations!

xxxviii►Don Stewart: What are some of the different titles of Satan? https://www.blueletterbible.org/faq/don_stewart/don_stewart_80.cfm, Accessed 15, Jun 2015.

xxxix ► Paraphrased: 1 Peter 5:8 (NKJV) 8 Be sober, be vigilant; because your adversary the devil walks about like a roaring lion, seeking whom he may devour.

xl ► Story of Lucifer-His status: https://www.allaboutgod.com/story-of-lucifer.htm, Accessed 15 June 2019.

xli ► The Mark of the Beast Explained: http://www.markbeast.com/satan/history-of-satan.htm, Accessed 15, June 2019.

xlii ► 2 Corinthians 4:4 (NIV) The god of this age has blinded the minds of unbelievers, so that they cannot see the light of the gospel that displays the glory of Christ, who is the image of God.

xliii ► Colossians 2:14-15 (NIV) 14 having canceled the charge of our legal indebtedness, which stood against us and condemned us; He has taken it away, nailing it to the cross. 15 And having disarmed the powers and authorities, He made a public spectacle of them, triumphing over them by the cross.

xliv ► 1 Peter 5:8 (AMP) 8 Be sober [well balanced and self-disciplined], be alert and cautious at all times. That enemy of yours, the devil, prowls around like a roaring lion [fiercely hungry], seeking someone to devour.

xlv ►Ryan LeStrange, Hell's Toxic Trio: Defeat the demonic spirits that stall your destiny, Charisma House, pp141.

xlvi ► Emotional Incest: https://psychcentral.com/blog/emotional-incest-when-is-close-too-close/, Accessed 15 Jun 2019.

xlvii ►Gary H. Lovejoy, Ph. D., A Pastor's guide for the shadow of depression, Wesleyan Publishing House 2014, pp.10

xlviii ►Gary H. Lovejoy, Ph. D.,, A Pastor's guide for the shadow of depression, Wesleyan Publishing House 2014, pp.11

xlix ►Gary H. Lovejoy, Ph. D.,, A Pastor's guide for the shadow of depression, Wesleyan Publishing House 2014, pp.11

l ► Complex Regional Pain Syndrome: https://www.mayoclinic.org/diseases-conditions/complex-regional-pain-syndrome/symptoms-causes/syc-20371151, Accessed 16 Jun 2019.

li ► James Maloney - Mark Chironna, The Panoramic Seer: Bringing the Prophetic into the Healing Anointing, Destiny Image Publishers, Inc.-2012, pp. 31.

lii ► Dark night of the soul by Eckhart Tolle, https://www.eckharttolle.com/eckhart-on-the-dark-night-of-the-soul/, Accessed 16, Jan 2019

liii ► AJ, Jones, Finding Father, XP Publishing 2012, pp. 67

liv ► Matthew 3:7 (NIV) 7 But when he saw many of the Pharisees and Sadducees coming to where he was baptizing, he said to them: "You brood of vipers! Who warned you to flee from the coming wrath?

lv ► 1 Kings 18:4a (NIV) 4 While Jezebel was killing off the Lord's Prophets.

lvi ► John 1:42 (TPT) 42 Then Andrew brought Simon to meet Him. When Jesus gazed upon Andrew's brother, He prophesied to him, "You are Simon and your father's name is Joh. But from now on you will be called Cephas" (which means, Peter the Rock).

lvii ► John 21:17 (NIV) 17 The third time he said to him, "Simon son of John, do you love me?" Peter was hurt because Jesus asked him the third time, "Do you love me?" He said, "Lord, you know all things; you know that I love you." Jesus said, "Feed my sheep.

lviii ► 2 Timothy 1:7 (KJV) 7 For God hath not given us the spirit of fear; but of power, and of love, and of a sound mind.

lix ► behind the name: Hamon: https://www.behindthename.com/element/hamon, Accessed 18 Jun 2019.

lx ► Nick Griemsmann, Defeating Mental Illness, Westbow Press 2018, p.19.

lxi ► https://www.biblestudytools.com/dictionary/heart/, Accessed 31 Dec 2018.

lxii ► https://www.hebrew4christians.com/Names_of_G-d/Adonai/adonai.html, Accessed 10 Jan 2019.

lxiii ► Always have open communication between The Holy Spirit and your doctor. The Lord will use any means necessary to heal you. For example, He might use your doctor.

lxiv ► https://www.desiringgod.org/articles/satans-go-to-temptation-against-you, Access 14 Jan 2019

lxv ► Mary K Baxter Ministries: http://www.marykbaxterinc.com/, Accessed 21 June 2019.

lxvi ► Bill Wiese Ministries: https://soulchoiceministries.org/, Accessed 21 June 2019.

lxvii ► https://www.myjewishlearning.com/article/serah-daughter-of-asher/, Accessed 16, Jan 2019

lxviii ► The Hebrew Midrash is a form of storytelling to bridge the gap between the law (Torah) and the timeless application.
https://www.myjewishlearning.com/article/midrash-101/, Accessed 16, Jan 2019

lxix ► James Maloney, The Panoramic Seer: Bringing the Prophetic into the Healing Anointing, Answering the Cry Publications – 2012, p. 81.

lxx ► Sermon quote from Derek Prince

lxxi ► Dr. Roger Sapp, Beyond A Shadow Of A Doubt, All Nations Publications 2001, pp. 81

lxxii ► Richard Foster, Celebration of Discipline: the Path to Spiritual Growth, Harpersanfrancisco-2003.

lxxiii ► Dr. Joan Hunter, Healing Starts Now! Complete Training Manual, Destiny Image Publishers, INC 2011, pp. 33.

lxxiv ►https://www.tomorrowsworld.org/booklets/does-god-heal-today/content, Accessed 23, Jan 2019.

lxxv ►https://www.tomorrowsworld.org/booklets/does-god-heal-today/content, Accessed 23 Jan 2019.

lxxvi ►https://www.tomorrowsworld.org/booklets/does-god-heal-today/content, Accessed 23, Jan 2019.

lxxvii ► 1 Timothy 5:23 (NKJV) 23 No longer drink only water, but use a little wine for your stomach's sake and your frequent infirmities.

lxxviii ► 2 Timothy 4:20 (NKJV) 20 Erastus stayed in Corinth, but Trophimus I have left in Miletus sick.

lxxix ► Jose Gonzalez Q., Transformed by the Spirit, Xulon Press 2010, pp. 200

lxxx ► "What are Strong's numbers?",
http://kingjamesbibledictionary.com/StrongsNumbers, Accessed 19, Jun 2019.

lxxxi ► https://biblehub.com/hebrew/6038.htm, Accessed 09, Feb 2019.

lxxxii ► Ryan LeStrange, Hells Toxic Trio: Defeat the Demonic Spirits That Stall Your Destiny, Charisma House 2018, pp.90

lxxxiii ► Ezekiel 36:26 (NIV) 26 I will give you a new heart and put a new spirit in you; I will remove from you your heart of stone and give you a heart of flesh.

lxxxiv ► Colossians 3:7-10 (TPT) 7-8 That's how you once behaved, characterized by your evil deeds. But now it's time to eliminate them from your lives once and for all – anger, fits of rage, all forms of hatred, cursing, filthy speech, 9 and lying. Lay aside your old Adam-self with its masquerade and disguise. 10 For you have acquired new creation life which is continually being renewed into the likeness of the One who created you; giving you the full revelation of God.

lxxxv ► Acts 7:58 (TPT) 58 Then they pounced on him and threw him outside the city walls to stone him. His accusers, one by one, placed their outer garments at the feet of a young man named Saul of Tarsus.

lxxxvi ► Celebrate Recovery ⊢ https://www.celebraterecovery.com/, Accessed 14 Mar 2019.
Find a group near you: https://locator.crgroups.info/

lxxxvii ►William Backus, The Hidden Rift With God, Bethany House Publishers 1990, pp. 21.

lxxxviii ► Sozo: Saved, Healed, Delivered by Bethel ⊢ http://bethelsozo.com/, Accessed 14 Mar 2019.

lxxxix ► https://www.whatchristianswanttoknow.com/what-is-biblical-counseling/, Accessed 14 October 2019.

xc ► Gary R. Collins, Ph.D., Helping Others Turn Potential Into Reality Christian Coaching, People Helper's International, Inc, 2001, pp 16.

xci ► Proverbs 27:17 (NIV) 17 As iron sharpens iron, so one person sharpens another.

xcii ► Colossians 3:16 (NIV) 16 Let the message of Christ dwell among you richly as you teach and admonish one another with all wisdom through psalms, hymns, and songs from the Spirit, singing to God with gratitude in your hearts.

xciii ► Lonely ⊢ https://www.merriam-webster.com/dictionary/lonely, Accessed 20 March 2019.

xciv ► Desolate ⊢ https://www.merriam-webster.com/dictionary/desolate, Accessed 20 March 2019.

xcv►Shabbath⊢ https://www.blueletterbible.org/lang/lexicon/lexicon.cfm?Strongs=H7673&t=KJV, Accessed 20 March 2019.

xcvi►Sunday Service For Christians Blue Letter Explanation ⊢
https://www.blueletterbible.org/faq/sabbath.cfm, Accessed 20 March 2019.

xcvii ► Jamie Buckingham, Daughter of Destiny The Only Authorized Biography Kathryn Kuhlman, Bridge-Logos 1999, pp. 53

xcviii►faith: https://www.merriam-webster.com/dictionary/faith, Accessed 31 October 2019.

xcix►Kabod ⊢ https://www.blueletterbible.org/lang/lexicon/lexicon.cfm?t=kjv&strongs=h3519, Accessed 17 Apr 2019

c ► Decree ⊢ https://biblehub.com/hebrew/1881.htm, Accessed 17 Apr 2019; also Strong's #633, 1504, 1697, 1881, 1882, 2706, 2710, 2940, 2942, 3982, 6599, 1378.

ci► Declare ⊢ https://biblehub.com/greek/5346.htm, Accessed 17 Apr 2019; also Strong's # 560, 874, 952, 1696, 3045, 5046, 5608, 7878, 8085, 312, 518, 1107, 1213, 1334, 1555, 1718, 1732. 2097, 2605, 3853, 5419.

cii► Success ⊢ https://www.compellingtruth.org/Bible-success.html, Accessed 17 Apr 2019

ciii► Sanctified ⊢
 https://www.biblestudytools.com/dictionary/sanctification/, Accessed 17 Apr 2019

civ► Offense ⊢ https://www.biblestudytools.com/dictionary/offence-offend/, Accessed 17 Apr 2019

cv► Authority ⊢ https://www.biblestudytools.com/dictionary/authority/, Accessed 17 Apr 2019

cvi► Sheol ⊢ https://www.biblestudytools.com/dictionary/sheol/, Accessed 17 Apr 2019

cvii► Righteousness ⊢ https://www.biblestudytools.com/dictionary/righteousness/, Accessed 17 Apr 2019

cviii ► Abba ⊢ https://biblehub.com/greek/5.htm, Accessed 17 Apr 2019

cix ► äb-bä ⊢ https://www.blueletterbible.org/lang/lexicon/lexicon.cfm?t=kjv&strongs=g5, Accessed 15 Jun 2019.

cx ► YHVH ⊢ https://www.conformingtojesus.com/hebrew_name_of_god_yhwh_meaning.htm, Accessed 17 Apr 2019

cxi ► Yĕhovah ⊢ https://www.blueletterbible.org/lang/lexicon/lexicon.cfm?t=kjv&strongs=h3068, Accessed 15 Jun 2019.

cxii ► Elohim ⊢ http://www.hebrew-streams.org/works/hebrew/context-elohim.html, Accessed 17 Apr 2019

cxiii ► el·ō·hēm ⊢ https://www.studylight.org/lexicons/hebrew/430.html, Accessed 15 Jun 2019.

cxiv ► Adonai ⊢ https://www.preceptaustin.org/adonai-lord-the_name_of_god, Accessed 17 Apr 2019

cxv ► ad·ō·nōy ⊢ https://www.blueletterbible.org/lang/lexicon/lexicon.cfm?t=kjv&strongs=h136, Accessed 15 Jun 2019.

cxvi ► Kyrios ⊢ https://www.bibliatodo.com/en/names-of-God/kyrios, Accessed 17 Apr 2019

cxvii ► kü'-rē-os ⊢ https://www.blueletterbible.org/lang/lexicon/lexicon.cfm?t=kjv&strongs=g2962, Accessed 15 Jun 2019.

cxviii ► Jehova Rapha ⊢ https://www.preceptaustin.org/jehovah_rophi_-_god_who_heals, Accessed 04 Apr 2020.

cxix ► Yâhh ⊢ https://www.blueletterbible.org/lang/lexicon/lexicon.cfm?t=kjv&strongs=h3050, Accessed 17 Apr 2019

cxx ► yä ⊢ https://www.blueletterbible.org/lang/lexicon/lexicon.cfm?t=kjv&strongs=h3050, Accessed 15 Jun 2019.

cxxi ► ruach ⊢ https://biblehub.com/hebrew/7307.htm, Accessed 24 July 2019.

cxxii►ruach phonetics:https://www.blueletterbible.org/lang/lexicon/lexicon.cfm?t=kjv&strongs=h7307, Accessed 24 July 2019.

cxxiii ► Spirit ⊢ http://www.hebrew-streams.org/works/spirit/ruachpneuma.html, Accessed 24 July 2019.

cxxiv ► John 14:6 (TPT) 6 Jesus explained, "I am the Way, I am the Truth, and I am the life. No one comes next to the Father except through union with me. To know me is to know my Father too.

cxxv ► Jesus phonetics: https://biblespeak.org/jesus-pronunciation/, Accessed 24 July 2019.

cxxvi ► Jesus the Messiah: https://www.jewishvoice.org/read/blog/yeshua-hamashiach-anointed-save, Accessed 22 August 2019.

www.ingramcontent.com/pod-product-compliance
Lightning Source LLC
LaVergne TN
LVHW051052080426
835508LV00019B/1828